Mindset Matters

*Developing mental agility and
resilience to thrive in uncertainty*

Gemma Leigh Roberts

KoganPage

First published in Great Britain and the United States in 2022 by Kogan Page Limited

2nd Floor, 45 Gee Street	8 W 38th Street, Suite 902	4737/23 Ansari Road
London	New York, NY 10018	Daryaganj
EC1V 3RS	USA	New Delhi 110002
United Kingdom		India
www.koganpage.com		

© Gemma Leigh Roberts 2022

ISBNs
Hardback   9781398605190
Paperback   9781398604841
Ebook   9781398605183

British Library Cataloguing-in-Publication Data
A CIP record for this book is available from the British Library.

Library of Congress Control Number
2022934099

Typeset by Hong Kong FIVE Workshop
Print production managed by Jellyfish
Printed and bound by CPI Group (UK) Ltd, Croydon CR0 4YY

Kogan Page books are printed on paper from sustainable forests.

CONTENTS

FIGURES AND TABLES

EXTRA RESOURCES

There is extra material to support what's in this book on my website **www.GemmaLeighRoberts/ MindsetMatters.com**. I'll remind you about it each time it comes up.

Introduction

It feels like change has become the only constant in our working lives, or perhaps that's life in general. We live in a fast-paced, constantly evolving world of work, and with that comes uncertainty. It's often during uncertain and changeable situations that we witness positive outcomes, such as the rise of new opportunities, creativity and innovation. But uncertainty often comes with challenges, unpredictability and discomfort. Why is it, then, that some people thrive in uncertainty, and others get stuck?

The short answer is that it's often to do with mindset – how we process information and view the world. As we'll explore in this book, there is more than one way to look at the world, and to process events that occur around us.

One person's problem is another person's puzzle to solve. An obstacle can be viewed as an opportunity if you choose to see it that way.

This doesn't mean those that thrive in uncertainty aren't realistic about the challenges they face, or they find the experience of change a completely comfortable place to be – often far from it. Those that thrive in unpredictable situations have learned strategies that help them to process, manage and use information in a way that enables them to keep moving forward, even when times are tough and they feel overwhelmed.

If you feel that you need some support and guidance in how to navigate the new world of work, I can categorically tell you you're not alone. This book started out as a newsletter on LinkedIn, and within 11 months of its launch 250,000 people had subscribed. Just over 18 months later that had jumped to 500,000 subscribers and the newsletter was one of the fastest growing on the LinkedIn platform. This is how I know you're not alone if you're interested in learning more about setting your mindset up for success. Hundreds of thousands of people around the world are looking for the same information. Remember that on the days when you feel like you're the only person who doesn't know how to navigate uncertainty, or what steps to take next. I promise you, you're not.

Your coaching guide

This book is a practical guide, created to help you navigate the new world of work. Five key mindset skills that *everyone* needs to thrive in the new world of work are explored, including: resilience, cognitive flexibility, growth mindset, emotional intelligence, and connection. In each topic area, I'll delve into topical research, and provide case studies and practical advice to help you master these skills in your working life (and often demystify the concept). I'll also share coaching techniques and strategies you can use to develop these skills – taking you from theory (which is interesting) to application (which can be transformative).

I'll share my expertise as a chartered psychologist in occupational psychology, an area I've been researching and working within for well over a decade. I've coached CEOs, leaders, executives, entrepreneurs, sales teams and graduates through more change than we ever could have predicted (think global financial crisis and pandemics), and as a resilience researcher I've become an expert in helping people to navigate and become comfortable with uncertainty.

This isn't an academic book, however; you won't need a Master's in psychology to understand the concepts or coaching techniques. My job is to translate often complex psychological research into practical, simple and evidence-based techniques that everyone can use to learn how to thrive in their career. I live and breathe this work and research, but I'm also a normal person running a business, and I think about what works for me and for others that I coach. Understanding the research is essential if you want to make effective changes in your life, but you must also be mindful of how that works in the real world – which is why there is such a focus on the practical application of strategies in this book. Equally, there is some great advice out there, and in some respects it doesn't matter where the information comes from if it's helpful for you. But if you're looking to develop several skills that will be the cornerstone of how you manage and navigate your career in the future, I believe it should be evidence-based and backed by research. This book is a happy medium – grounded in academia, but practical and simple enough to be applied by everyone, in all working contexts, no matter where you are on your career journey.

Work today

If you don't feel like you're thriving right now in your working life, you're not doing it 'wrong'. We all feel this at times, myself included. You may have experienced burnout, whereby you feel exhausted, overwhelmed and stressed at work. Maybe you've found yourself languishing in your career, which psychologist Adam Grant has described as feeling joyless and aimless.[1] The truth is, you won't always be thriving in your career; no one feels at the top of their game all the time, always performing at their peak. But you can have moments of thriving, and you want those when it really matters, such as when you're facing a huge challenge that could either be a career opportunity, or derail it. Or you're pushing yourself to take the next step in your career, and you want to find ways to effectively deal with the pressure and perform.

This book isn't about where I think the world is heading, although I talk about that in some places. And I don't want to tell you how you should feel about your work or the challenges you face. This is *your* coaching manual. It has been written to empower you, and to provide you with useful tools to navigate your unique and individual working life. Honestly, you don't need me, or any other expert, to tell you what to do. What you need is to find your own way to master uncertainty confidently, with support, and with guidance you can trust. I encourage you to claim your mindset journey, take control of your direction, and use this book in a way that works for you.

Theory + coaching

The ideas and suggestions in this book are not definitive. There isn't one way to create a mindset that sets you up for success. I encourage you to experiment with the coaching exercises and test what works for you. I talk a lot about developing an experimental mindset, and that's exactly what you need when figuring out how to navigate changes and challenges. Treat it as an experiment – test an approach, gather feedback, reflect on how it's worked, and make tweaks to the approach, so the strategies work even better for you in the future. How we think, process information and interact with the world has the potential to be ever-evolving, so you may find the way you manage your mindset continually develops. I wholeheartedly welcome alternative perspectives and ideas, so please don't feel restricted by these coaching exercises – adapt the exercises to suit you or skip to the strategies you want to test.

You'll find each topic has two chapters dedicated to it. The first is full of case studies, research, real-life examples and insights. The second is a collection of coaching exercises and strategies that will help you to develop that particular mindset or skill. Navigate these chapters in a way that works for you.

My Mindset Matters resources

I recommend before you do anything else, download your free Mindset Matters assessment from my website (see page 1).

This will provide you with a personalized overview of where you might want to focus your energy and attention when it comes to nurturing a mindset that sets you up for success, and you can use this information as a guide to help you work through the tools and resources in this book.

Getting the most out of this book

There are five topics explored in this book, each of which is an important component of thriving at work today:

1 Resilience
2 Cognitive flexibility
3 Growth mindset
4 Emotional intelligence
5 Connection

Each has two chapters dedicated to it. The first explores the topic, delving into real-life examples, case studies, research and observations, so you build a solid under-standing of how that mindset element plays a role in helping you to thrive in uncertainty. The second chapter on the topic is full of coaching strategies and exercises. This is your practical toolkit to help you apply the principles you're learning about.

You can work through the chapters in a way that works for you – you might explore the book from cover to cover, or you may dip into the topics that resonate with you. The Mindset Matters assessment tool might help you to decide the order in which you focus on these topics. You can download it from my website (see page 1).

I wish you the best of luck on your journey of learning more about your own mindset and creating a mindset that sets you up for success. My hope is this book becomes a resource you can easily work through to help you navigate change, challenges and uncertainty at work, helping you to create a positive, fulfilling and healthy working life.

CHAPTER 01

We've come a long way

In 2019, the world changed in ways we could never have predicted. The Covid-19 pandemic swiftly reached every corner of our planet and it felt like the world as we knew it came grinding to a halt. We didn't know it then, but our working lives were about to change forever. Virtual working became the norm for many people, and employees struggled to manage isolation, loss of physical connection with their teams, the pressures of caregiving at the same time as working, and the fear of what was to come. People started to crave connection and direction, both of which were a long way off at the start of the pandemic. In reality, no one knew what to do and how to handle the situation most effectively – not CEOs, board directors, leaders. Not even our governments. In this respect, we were all in our own individual boats out at sea (some more robust and sea-worthy than others), but ultimately, everyone was experiencing the exact same storm, struggling to find a direction and at times keep afloat.

If you worked through this, the chances are you experienced all kinds of emotions in your working life that you might not have experienced before. If you weren't part of the workforce as the world lived through this extreme change, there's no doubt you'll be working in a world that is dealing with the after-effects, which could change the way we work for decades to come.

Working in a volatile, uncertain, complex and ambiguous environment

In reality, we were already living in an unpredictable and ever-changing working world before the pandemic. In fact, the rise of conversations on how to navigate a volatile, uncertain, complex and ambiguous (VUCA) environment had already been penetrating boardrooms and leadership conferences around the world since the late 1990s. If we look back at the last 20 years of work, change and uncertainty had become the norm. Remote work increased, and the rise of the gig economy made working life more flexible for many people, but this also came with challenges as new ways of working that support remote collaboration needed to be scoped out, and it took time for fair and equitable employment rights to become the norm for those in the gig economy. Arguably, there's a lot more progress to be made.

Over the past decade technology has aided a more productive working life. Consider the rise of the BlackBerry and iPhone; all positive developments, as we can respond on the move and remain connected with more ease than ever. Until it wasn't so positive, of course, and a generation of employees started to suffer the effects of burnout and stress associated with an 'always on' culture, where responses to emails at the weekends or at 11pm became expected. We may have started to understand the benefits of a digital detox and having time to switch off from work, but how many people do you know that check their emails before they've even got out of bed in the morning? In fact, email has such an impact on burnout that France implemented a law in 2016 that restricts email communication outside of working hours within companies that employ over 50 people, and Portugal followed suit with a similar law in 2021.[1]

For the first time ever, up to five generations are working together. This historic development is a positive one, promoting a diverse workplace when it comes to age, as multiple generations with varied and diverse experience and expertise all work side-by-side. This is a clear reminder that the global workforce is constantly changing and evolving as new generations join the workforce, with different perspectives, objectives and values. Of course, you probably can't help but notice the increased focus on the desire to find meaning in the workplace, and align workplace values with personal values. Today, we want our work to mean something to us. In what has been an employee's recruitment market for so long – where people have options about the type of work they do and where they work – and in the age of wellbeing and bringing your whole authentic self to work, now more than ever employees are motivated by meaningful work. Partly the focus on finding meaning in work has been a reaction to stress, burnout and anxiety, where meaningful working is described as an antidote to the negative impacts of long hours, increased pressure and fewer resources.[2]

As the demands and priorities within organizations change, the workforce morphs to support business objectives and desired outcomes. As the demographics, needs and desires of the global workforce advance, corporate values and objectives transform to meet these. If there's one thing history teaches us about the workplace, it's that continual evolution is to be expected.

Navigating a pandemic at work

It's clear our working environments were shifting pre-Covid-19, and it's easy to get caught up in the accelerated changes the pandemic caused. But let's be realistic – our working lives will always be evolving and transforming. Navigating a pandemic did, however, create deeper and wider shockwaves in our working lives than we would have experienced had we not had to deal with such extreme change.

When the Covid-19 pandemic hit, for many of us our working lives were forced to become flexible, at speed. Overnight, office workers replaced commuting to offices with working at a kitchen table alongside other family members or those they share living space with. People who normally travelled as part of their work had to replace face-to-face meetings with video conference calls, and those that still worked with the general public had to get used to new safety measures, procedures and restrictions. Although challenges and change are inevitable at work, the speed at which the working population had to respond and adapt was unique. In 'normal' times the pace of change is slower, and we have more time to reflect on changes, strategically choose action steps, review progress and change course if necessary. In short, we have more time to learn. Collectively, we've had to rely on less tried and tested methods, and we've become more creative about connecting the dots and coming up with new ideas and potential strategies to solve problems; we've become more innovative by putting that creativity into action.

It's unlikely that anyone would have chosen the extreme workplace change and uncertainty faced in recent years, but globally we learned pretty quickly how to be agile. And the working world was already changing; we were already learning to adapt to changes and overcome challenges that come from operating in fast-paced and complex working environments, where the focus is on achieving more with less budget, resource or time. Whether you enjoy change or not, the chances are you've had to learn to become more adept at navigating it. The workplace today is nothing if not agile.

So now we need to focus on what's next for us at work. Although we can never know exactly what the future of work will look like, based on past patterns and the shifts we've seen in the workplace over the last decade, we can be sure it will involve change and uncertainty. The question we should all be asking ourselves today isn't 'How can I recover from the extreme change experienced?' Instead, we should ask, 'How can I prepare and equip myself to deal with change and challenges in the future?'

Dealing with change

You may have found yourself enduring relentless change, but how do you get to the position where you're truly thriving in change? Often, change is viewed as a threat rather than an opportunity, and with change comes risk, which is something many organizations have traditionally sought to avoid or minimize. As an employee or leader, change and risk can cause uncertainty as new situations unfold, and being unclear about how to move forward isn't always comfortable in a working environment that rewards those that are effective at attaining targets, displaying productivity and showcasing tangible outputs.

The question we should all be asking ourselves today isn't 'How can I recover from the extreme change experienced?' Instead, we should ask, 'How can I prepare and equip myself to deal with change and challenges in the future?'

But there can be a cost for not adapting to change. Take the example of Kodak, a company that originally developed a digital camera in the 1970s but fell far behind competitors decades later in the race to seize the digital photography market.[3] How could this happen? Senior executives at Kodak appreciated the creativity it took to design a digital camera, but they refused to believe or acknowledge digital photography was the future of the industry because that was an uncomfortable truth and a threat to the large film-based business that had turned Kodak into a hugely profitable company. Uncertainty and change can be uncomfortable, challenging and potentially disastrous if they are not addressed and appropriately managed.

The first step in thriving through change is to accept the new situation with flexibility and openness. Denying, ignoring or fighting change won't make it disappear, as executives at Kodak can attest to. Piyush Gupta, the CEO at Singapore's DSB bank, has taken a completely different approach to dealing with change as millennial employees started to become the largest part of the employee population. He has led the transformation from a traditional state bank to a tech company that focuses on banking, by embracing a start-up culture. Not only has this approach helped to stave off Chinese banking competition, it has also led to DBS being awarded World's Best Bank three years in a row, and culturally aligns with how millennials in the bank want to work.[4]

Whatever industry you work in, wherever you're located in the world, you will face change. Once you've accepted this fact, the next step is to find opportunities in the situation you find yourself in. It's often useful to understand risk appetite, both your own and within the organization you work for – ideally you want these to be aligned. If your risk appetite is low but the organization you work for requires or expects you to take risks, this can pose a challenge. You may appreciate more time to work through challenges methodically and to take your time to come up with a response, whereas your company may embrace disruption and swift action when it comes to dealing with challenges. The opposite scenario, whereby you're ready and willing to work through change quickly but the organization you work for is more conservative in the approach to risk, may leave you feeling stifled and stunted when it comes to dealing with challenges or navigating new developments within your industry. People who thrive on change share common attributes – they're flexible and open-minded in how they approach change and the challenges that are thrown their way.

Netflix is a great example of a company that has constantly adapted to changing circumstances. It has successfully shifted its business model several times to align with consumer demands and advancements in technology – and grown exponentially because of it. The company started in 1997 as a mail-order DVD rental company, pivoted to a video streaming platform in 2007, and soon became a distributor of original content. Today Netflix is a complete media company that has won Academy Awards. This constant adaptation has been led by a flexible and agile culture promoted by CEO Reed Hastings, and embraced across the organization, from new joiners to directors.[5] This willingness to recognize when its business model was at risk of becoming obsolete due to where the world was heading, and completely reinvent itself according to the needs of the market, is what has allowed the company to thrive. It has been able to do this because of its commitment to listening to its users – continuously analysing user data and then letting this steer strategy. Instead of being product-driven, Netflix realized early on that the need it was serving was helping people find and access great film and television entertainment, not to build a better DVD rental company, or even, later, streaming service. Take a moment to consider how you respond to new developments in your business or industry. Do you embrace new ways of moving forward and find ways to pivot? Or is your first response to new developments to stay on the same path and adapt your plan?

If Netflix had remained fixed on their original operational strategy, they would still be distributing DVDs and would likely have become obsolete, as witnessed during the demise of Blockbuster. In the 1990s Blockbuster employed 84,000 employees across the globe and boasted 65 million worldwide customers.[6] At that stage it would be hard for customers to imagine a world without the rental store, and executives within the business would have no doubt agreed. The problem for Blockbuster was that it failed to respond to changes in customer needs and desires – customers who were embracing the Netflix approach of supplying entertainment straight to their homes through a mail delivery system and enjoying the subscription model rather than paying to rent each DVD. To add salt to the wound, Blockbuster turned down a $50 million deal to purchase Netflix.

Do you embrace new ways of moving forward and find ways to pivot? Or is your first response to new developments to stay on the same path and adapt your plan?

It's easy to assume executives at Blockbuster were ignor-
ant of the impact the Netflix distribution model was having
on the home entertainment market, but this isn't the case.
Company reports filed by Blockbuster note Netflix as a
threat to their competitive strategy, and Blockbuster was
endeavouring to start a subscription service in a deal with
Enron that didn't work out. Unfortunately for the future
of Blockbuster, the technology they were using wasn't
effective and Enron went bust. Another factor that led to
the decline of Blockbuster was the reliance on late fees as
a revenue stream, something that Blockbuster were reluctant to let go of, and can't be replicated with a subscription
model. When Blockbuster did eventually offer a mail order
option alongside their store offering, it was more expen-
sive than Netflix, most likely because of the store costs.
Blockbuster just didn't make the shift to an online business
quickly enough and evolve from the store distribution
model which had built the empire.

It's not the case that Blockbuster failed to pivot their
strategy – rather, Blockbuster didn't pivot *quickly enough*,
and, most importantly, they didn't readjust their strategy
into streaming when the deal with Enron didn't work out.
In some ways, Blockbuster was trying to be adaptable, but
it just didn't move swiftly with momentum.

When we hear stories like this, unless you're the CEO
of multimillion-dollar business, it can feel distant and
irrelevant to your life. But these high-profile lessons are
there for you to learn from. Rather than learning only
from your own experiences, it's a smart move to also learn
from others.

You may be just starting out in your career, or you may be leading a team. Wherever you are right now on your career journey take a moment to pause and consider how you feel about change. Does the idea of transformation fill you with dread? Are you open to new ideas and curious to try new ways of doing things? If you feel that you embrace change, are you able to bring others along on the ride with you? The future of work will be fast-moving as new technologies such as artificial intelligence, automation and robotics develop. Embracing change and adapting will be core components of your future success at work.

No matter how open you are to change right now, if you can build strategic planning into your working life, you'll become more adept at not only preparing for the future but also predicting it.

Envisioning different versions of the future can be an effective way not only to cope with a changeable landscape, but actually to prepare yourself for potential changes and challenges that may come your way. Developing the ability to consider what future challenges and opportunities may impact your role, division or industry can minimize the uncomfortable uncertainty that can accompany change. We all have an appetite for experiencing change – some find the experience exciting and motivating, whereas others find the same situation unsettling and are fearful or anxious when they focus on the transformations that are happening around them. No matter how open you are to change right now, if you can build strategic planning into your working life, you'll become more adept at not only preparing for the future but also predicting it. Had Kodak taken this approach, and strategically mapped out risks, threats and opportunities associated with the rise of digital photography, rather than dismissing digital as an uncomfortable inconvenience, they may have taken a larger share of the digital market ahead of competitors.

When it comes to imagining what your future at work could look like, take the lead from Elon Musk, co-founder of PayPal, founder of SpaceX and CEO of Tesla. Ask yourself one simple question: 'How can I make things better?' Musk is a serial entrepreneur and innovator but he doesn't believe in translating new ideas into reality just to be different. In fact, he questions whether this is innovation at all. Rather, Musk implores his team to make a difference, to create a service or product that is better and delivers more value to people, organizations or the planet. When you work on envisioning your future, start with what you can do to make things better.

Of course, you can't control how the future pans out. Holding on to the hope you can completely direct your future by continuously thinking about it may create tension, and possibly feed into anxiety or stress. Taking time to consider how the future may unfold for you, your team, your business and industry can, however, provide some comfort if the idea of change can at times make you uneasy. The trick is to not allow thoughts about what may happen consume you, as that can cause worry or fear. Instead, map out strategy sessions periodically where you think through possibilities as you see developments unfold around you. Take into account industry, technology and economic developments and ask yourself how these could affect you. Where could the opportunities lie? Where could there be causes for concern? If these scenarios pan out, you will have some ideas about how to tackle the situation, but that isn't the point of this exercise. The reason this strategic thinking is so important is because it reinforces the idea that you *can* deal with change and challenges. In reality, the chances of the exact scenarios you envision playing out may be slim, but through this process you're developing and reinforcing a cognitive skill required to deal with change effectively – considering your options and opportunities objectively.

In the age of disruption and working in a fast-paced, competitive environment, employees have been stripped of the luxury of psychological space to consider how to respond to events, and the time to reflect and plan. An obvious antidote to this may be to teach yourself how to be prepared for all eventualities, but this is practically impossible if employees are working at their capacity to achieve results in an ever-progressing work environment. The practical approach is to become adept at strategic and agile thinking, honing the skills required to deal with change as it comes, rather than fixating on what the future may look like, which in all honesty we can never know.

Rather than just working through ambiguity, get used to it. We work in a VUCA world – it's volatile, uncertain, complex and ambiguous. When you feel dread creeping in as you face challenges, before your mind goes anywhere else, focus on finding one opportunity that might arise from the situation and use that to give you hope. In March 2020 I was a few months into a doctorate programme with a new baby and a two-year-old child, and my husband,

Jake, was two months into a dream job with a company he'd just joined, something he'd been working towards for a long time. Within a week, he was on furlough and never returned to the company. His role was to implement strategic plans to grow the business, but this had been wiped out by a pandemic – there were no future plans, it was all about survival for the business. As my husband called with the news, I was about to walk around a lake with our new baby, and our eldest little girl was at nursery. Jake met us, and we walked around that lake in the spring sunshine, him in his suit and tie, me in my gym gear. We looked like we were in different lives, him suited and booted and me in my active wear. And, in all honesty, our lives were about to look very different.

Of course, Jake was bitterly disappointed and concerned about the volatility of the situation and what that meant for our family, and I felt that too. But overwhelmingly I felt like this was an opportunity for us. My area of research is psychological resilience, and I knew with the extreme change we were all about to face the whole world would need to focus on building psychological resilience. I knew that I was going to be busy, and in that moment I also knew I wouldn't get the maternity leave I had planned and so desperately wanted after returning to work after four months off with my first baby, which had felt too soon as I looked back. So, I posed the question, 'Why don't you work with me and grow the business?' This is a scenario I'd always imagined would happen some day, and I had visions of Jake taking over the operational and strategic activities (which leave me in a cold sweat) and I would lead the research, content, design and delivery – which is where my expertise lies. But I absolutely did not feel ready for this scenario before we were hit with a pandemic to navigate.

I would love to tell you it's been plain sailing, but it has been far from it. We've had to figure out how to work together, parent together, be married and all while we've had long periods of all being in the house together. It's been a baptism of fire, and some of the best of times, and worst of times. But when a situation hit that could have been a disaster, I took the optimistic approach and focused on what may be a once in a lifetime opportunity. We adapted quickly, we learned from the many, many mistakes that followed. We pivoted (repeatedly) and just kept tweaking until it all started to work.

I know that sounds like a unique experience, but everyone's story is unique. In reality you most likely won't face the same challenges as someone else, and you may not have the exact same opportunities available to you. But rather than listen to other people's stories and think about how interesting it is, think instead what you can learn from someone else's experience and how you can apply that to your life to drive positive change.

When you're ready to take the next step in navigating your change journey, being adaptable in how you think about the situation and agile in your problem-solving approach are principles that will help you to effectively work through uncertainty.

What does it mean to be mentally agile?

The concept of mental agility is born out of research into the areas of learning agility, psychological resilience and innovation, and has become a key skill required to navigate today's workplace. Mental agility refers to being flexible in responding to events and new situations, while moving between ideas nimbly and quickly. When you're mentally agile, you'll be comfortable with complexity. You'll be effective at thinking on your feet and solving problems, and you'll grasp new ideas and concepts that help you to find new and innovative solutions.

Those that are mentally agile have a unique skill whereby they take a curious approach to life, taking pleasure from learning about novel ideas and new innovations, not only within their current circle of knowledge or area of expertise, but also in completely unrelated areas. Consider the sales director who takes online courses in areas such as photography, writing and interior design for no other reason than those topics being of interest. Or the HR manager who works in Singapore and has a subscription to the *New Yorker*.

Mental agility can be described as connecting not so obvious dots. When the Macintosh computer was unveiled in 1984, it included many new features the likes of which had never been seen before. Perhaps one of the most overlooked of these features with regards to innovative outputs was the inclusion of a variety of fonts in the word processing application. Today it's hard to imagine life in one font, but that was the norm before Steve Jobs created fonts. But how did Jobs come up with this idea? It all stemmed from a calligraphy class he took at Reed College, a class which he joined for no other reason than interest in the topic. Jobs had never intended to be a calligrapher – he wasn't learning the skills to help him on his future career path, or to pass an exam to get to the next professional development step. He was fascinated with the art of hand drawing letters and simply found the process of calligraphy intriguing.

Fast-forward a decade and that fateful class resulted in Jobs designing a multitude of new fonts for the Macintosh computer system. Often when we think about connecting dots between ideas, we imagine ideas within the same context forming new pathways to push forward existing knowledge or outputs. At times, this is how mental agility works. But there are also situations where completely unconnected ideas merge to form new concepts. Take, for example, Pierre Omidyar, the founder of eBay, who connected the dots between the launch of the internet and his partner's collection of PEZ dispensers, which were difficult to find and purchase. He found a way to bypass classified adverts, which were ineffective, and built the e-commerce website that we now know as eBay. Omidyar was able to move between very diverse ideas and concepts and build a solution to the problem of his fiancée's challenge in sourcing new collectable items, and in the process he created a service that would go on to become one of the largest e-commerce platforms ever created.

Of course, day-to-day we may not be creating new businesses or global e-commerce platforms, but some of the same skills apply to thriving in uncertainty whether you're a CEO of a start-up, managing a marketing team or taking the first steps in your career. If you can learn to become more comfortable with uncertainty, you're more likely to find opportunities when facing obstacles and, rather than avoid the situation, find a way to quickly and effectively tackle the challenge head-on.

Problem solving is a key component of mental agility, and there is a way to hone problem-solving ability. When facing challenges, rather than adopt the first viable response you consider, pause and take time to consider all viable options. You might get lucky and come up with a great solution immediately, but you might not. There could be an even better response, which unless you take the time to consider alternative options, and potentially garner feedback and suggestions from others, you'll never know. As you practise thinking broadly rather than focusing on one possible response, you'll learn the skills required to grasp new ideas quickly and push through complexity, which are both factors that support mental agility.

Often, we think of ourselves either as someone who likes detail, or as someone who takes a broader strategic view – one or the other. Traditionally, personality assessments have pitched these two approaches to interpreting data against each other – you're either a detailed or a strategic person. This may be the case, you may have a preference towards one or the other; the majority of people certainly do. But if you want to develop mental agility it's important to know you can develop other ways to interpret information, and honing the ability to switch between being a micro (detail) and macro (strategic) thinker is an essential skill in today's workplace.

You may be a strategic thinker with the ability to connect dots at ease, spot new trends and quickly adapt your objectives to align with a changing environment around you. Or you may be someone that can take a strategic goal and create a robust and detailed plan to reach the target, considering project inter-dependencies, potential risks and opportunities. The point is you don't have to be one or the other, and you can learn how to think both in detail and strategically – which is ideal if you want to develop mental agility. If your thinking style aligns with strategic planning, you may find the details harder to grasp, which is something I've had to manage throughout my career. But over the years I've had to develop the skills required to focus on details. All of my jobs, from entry level to midway through my career, required attention to detail and it's something I still have to work on today. It may not be my natural way of thinking, but whenever I'm in strategic planning mode I immediately switch to focusing on the details, understanding exactly how to make the plans a reality and where the pitfalls may be, even though this isn't a comfortable process for me. And the same can be done if you want to hone your strategic thinking skills – it's a matter of taking the time to think through the bigger picture, potentially with a colleague, mentor or coach, and focusing on intentionally taking a step back from the details to get a broad picture.

When it comes to navigating change and practising mental agility, a key skill is communication. Sometimes leaders or experts feel the need to display their knowledge by detailing complex intricacies, but this is a guaranteed way to lose audience attention. In fact, a harder and more effective approach is to communicate complex ideas simply, and this is a skill that can be practised and developed. When you're explaining a new idea, challenge yourself to do so in as few words as possible, or use diagrams to illustrate your thoughts.

Learning to navigate change and develop mental agility are the first steps in learning to thrive in uncertainty. You may still have some further questions such as:

- How do I navigate the new working world effectively?
- How do I survive and thrive in extreme change?
- How can I direct my future at work?
- How do I face and overcome fear, feelings of being over-whelmed and exhaustion at work?
- How can I create my own opportunities to thrive at work?

We'll focus on these in the next chapter.

We have indeed come a long way in the world of work, and it's important to look back at how the working world has changed to identify lessons we can learn. Throughout the rest of this book, however, we'll focus on the key mindset skills you need not only to survive, but also to thrive in the workplace of today, and the future. In the next chapter we're going to jump right in to one of the most important skills you can master for career success today – resilience.

CHAPTER 02

Resilience

The focus on enhancing psychological resilience for employees within organizations has grown significantly over the last decade, particularly as we navigate challenging, changeable and complex workplace dynamics. As the world of work has become increasingly volatile, uncertain, complex and ambiguous, organizations have started to look at how leaders and employees can be equipped with the tools to navigate change and challenges in an unpredictable landscape, which often entails focusing on helping people to build psychological resilience.

Resilience could be a term you've come across recently – it's been a hot topic as we collectively dealt with disruption and change in the working world. But what exactly is resilience? And why is resilience so important?

The age of resilience

Definitions of psychological resilience can be so varied, it can be hard to determine exactly what resilience means, even in research literature. In short, psychological resilience is the ability to recover and grow from adversity. Which sounds simple, but what does it actually mean to be resilient?

To understand the evolution of psychological resilience, it might be helpful to take a whistle-stop tour of how the construct became such a focus, both in the workplace and in life in general. Early research focused on the process of children being exposed to stressors in early life and over-coming extreme adversity to function and even thrive in later life. Researchers wanted to know how this hap-pened, and what it was that meant some children thrived while others struggled following adversity. The answer was resilience.[1] Those that demonstrated resilience were much more likely to adapt and report positive outcomes later in life.

Research into resilience in adults followed, and studies identified a sweet spot in the relationship between experi-encing challenge and the ability to achieve goals, whereby those that face a certain amount of pressure learn to posi-tively adapt and grow from the experience, and those that face extreme amounts of stress, or no pressure at all, are less likely to develop resilience and report positive outcomes in the future. An example of this is a study of Vietnam War veterans, which found that those who experienced the war but were not directly exposed to combat had greater improvements in their psychological functioning later in life than those that experienced no direct exposure, or any exposure at all.[2]

As resilience research has progressed, an interest in resilience in the workplace has gained momentum, in particular in the area of helping employees to be more resilient to deal with change and challenges effectively. Which makes sense, when you consider that stress and burnout are on the rise in the workplace, and building resilience has been championed as an antidote. But building resilience can be a complicated process – you need some exposure to pressure, but not necessarily too much where the challenge becomes overwhelming. You need to take into account your environment and the context around you, considering factors such as building a strong support structure and working within an organization that not only supports the development of resilience, but provides you with the opportunity to find your own way to thrive in uncertainty.

Resilience is dynamic. The interaction between a person and their environment shapes the level of resilience experienced, and resilience reserves can change over the course of a lifetime. There are so many factors that could affect your resilience at this very moment – your personality, stress levels, the number of challenges you face right now, the challenges you've faced in the past, the intensity of pressure you're experiencing, your home situation, your work environment, your relationships with others. How these factors interact can affect your resilience reserves. It's easy to see how resilience has become a complex construct to decode and understand, but the truth of it is you can learn how to build your resilience to deal with uncertainty in the workplace. You just need to know where to start.

Why would you want to focus on enhancing your resilience, you may wonder. Resilience is a useful tool that can not only help to reduce stress in the moment but can buffer against future stress. This means resilience can help you to react to stress in a healthy way, reduce the side effects, and prevent future stress and burnout. People who are resilient report feeling more in control when dealing with obstacles and are more comfortable about navigating change. They're also more likely to tackle challenges head-on rather than avoiding uncomfortable situations. As the challenges we face in the working world become more frequent and complex, and reported cases of burnout at work are steadily rising, it's clear why focusing on resilience in the workplace is an essential part of your toolkit if you want to not only survive but also thrive at work.

Resilience is a useful tool that can not only help to reduce stress in the moment but can buffer against future stress.

Resilience at work

Although we can never predict the future of work entirely, we can observe trends, and it is clear that change and uncertainty are part of everyone's future at work. Building your resilience can help you to navigate changes and complexities in the workplace in a healthy way, particularly as the pressures of work and life are mounting. It's not surprising that the World Economic Forum reported in 2021 that learning and development professionals across the globe are identifying resilience and adaptability as *the* most important skills required at work.[3]

You may be wondering why exactly resilience is such a crucial trait in the workplace. This is because highly resilient individuals have the ability to push the boundaries of their skills and abilities, and test new ideas safe in the knowledge that if they should encounter failure, their high levels of resilience will allow them to overcome such adversity and bounce forward, growing and learning from the experience and building psychological strength to handle challenges in the future. These are skills we all need as we navigate the unpredictable future of work.

Resilient people help to create a more innovative organization, as they're more likely to test new ideas without encountering the paralysing fear of failure, and they can recover stronger when things don't go to plan, which is part and parcel of innovation. On an individual level, those that are more resilient report better wellbeing – which means boosting resilience can also help to reduce stress, burnout, anxiety and depression. Research has shown that resilient people have attributes that help to facilitate adjustment and coping in adverse or stressful situations, whereas someone with low resilience may struggle to cope with challenging situations such as failure, which can lead to negative emotions.[4]

Although the focus on resilience at work is becoming more prominent, there have been negative connotations associated with resilience in the past, for example false assumptions such as that focusing on resilience is only required if you're unable to cope with pressure. Recent research has debunked this myth, and as we learn more about how resilience works it has become clear that high-performing individuals are resilient. They don't experience less adversity – rather, they utilize strategies to enhance their resilience to find ways to overcome challenges effect-ively. In fact, a study found resilience resourcefulness – whereby an individual draws on their skills, abilities and the support of those around them in challenging situations – is one of the greatest predictors of entrepreneurial success.[5] Of course, entrepreneurs often experience extreme adver-sity, and they use resilience resources to deal with these situations effectively. You *high-performing* may not be an entrepreneur, but we can *individuals are* all learn from this approach in the workplace. You don't need to be an *resilient* entrepreneur to encounter stressful situ-ations and adversity and benefit from building your resilience reserves.

Resilience levels will change over time in different situations. Although a resilience journey can be tricky to conceptualize, think of your resilience as a reservoir – sometimes your levels will be higher, and sometimes your levels will be depleted. You needn't wait for a drought to start replenishing your reservoir; you can keep it topped up by maintaining and nurturing your resilience levels. If your reservoir is full when a drought hits you have resilience reserves to rely on. As is the case for water reservoirs, prolonged droughts will hit, and your resilience reserves may become dangerously low at times. No matter how diligent you are at strengthening, nurturing and maintaining your resilience levels, if you face multiple challenges at once, or you face an extreme threat, your resilience may become unhealthily impacted. The key to building your resilience is to understand the personal strategies that work for you.

Boosting resilience in a work context has been shown to reduce burnout, which is on the rise in the workplace. Resilient individuals can deal with adversity faster, with less negative impact on personal wellbeing. As your resilience reserves increase, so does the strength of relationships – with your team, boss, peers and clients. It becomes easier to navigate difficult conversations, deliver challenging feedback, digest feedback from others and use humility to offer and ask for support. In a fast-paced and constantly evolving workplace, resilience is an important factor in nurturing creativity and innovation. Resilient people find problem solving easier, they can challenge themselves to see situations from different perspectives, to move between different ideas quickly, and recover quicker when things don't go to plan, or they experience failure.

The six pillars of resilience

The construct of resilience can be complex to navigate. It can be tricky to know where to start when focusing on building and nurturing your resilience. At times you may need to rest and recover, sometimes you may benefit from focusing on regeneration and recharging. The ideal place to start when exploring your resilience is the six pillars that work together to build a snapshot of resilience:

1 Confidence
2 Adaptability
3 Positivity
4 Perspective
5 Mastery
6 Stamina

Confidence

When it comes to building resilient confidence, it's less about how you interact with others, and more about believing in your ability to solve problems and figure out next steps when you have no clue how to tackle a new challenge. It's also about understanding and playing to your unique strengths and getting clear on how to take control when faced with challenges.

Some organizations and individuals focus on the resilience pillar of confidence to support innovation exceptionally well. Take Spotify, for example, one of the leaders in disruptive innovation. Having transformed the music industry and how people listen to music, it has gone on to become the world's biggest music streaming platform. The business was one of the first to successfully implement the 'freemium' model and to use data-driven personalization to recommend music and curate tailored playlists to drive discovery and engagement. It also evolved with the market and consumer behaviour in recent years, making the most of popular technology and other platforms by integrating with social networks and dating apps, and offering social features such as shared links and playlists.

In late 2020, the business hit a roadblock. Because it has so many free users who must listen to adverts, it relied heavily on advertising revenue. However, companies were suddenly slashing budgets due to the pandemic. In response, Spotify pivoted – it began to offer original content in the vein of Netflix, signing exclusive podcast deals with several celebrities and curating radio shows. The strategy at Spotify was to find a way to take control of the situation, and even though the solution to rectify the issue of reduced revenue may not have been immediately obvious, there was a sense of inevitability that the solution could be identified, a belief in the collective ability to respond to problems.

Confidence can also protect against negative stressors, as highlighted in a 2012 study of Olympic champions.[6] It was found that confidence, focus and perceived social support were positively related to high levels of resilience and allowed Olympic champions to reframe potentially negative experiences and give them positive meaning. High levels of confidence and psychological resilience helped these athletes to attain optimal sport performance – which is something that can be replicated in the workplace. Focusing on confidence can help to enhance performance and master uncertainty. It's important to remember you don't need to have all the answers, you just need confidence in your ability to find a solution – either alone or with the help of a team or network.

Adaptability

In the past, researchers would often talk about bouncing back after facing adversity, but throughout my doctoral research it's become clear this is an oversimplified view of how resilience can support growth after facing a challenging situation. Suggesting that following trauma, to recover through resilience people should leave behind and forget about negative experiences and return to their pre-adversity state is a huge, missed opportunity. In coaching sessions, I often talk through the analogy of training for a marathon. Imagine you're increasing your running distance regularly, and when you reach the ten-mile mark in your training you injure yourself. If bouncing back from this unfortunate situation were the goal, you'd be happy to go through physiotherapy, rebuild your strength and get back to the ten-mile mark in your training. If, however, your goal was to bounce forward, you would want to learn from your experience, understand how you could adjust your technique so you're not injured again in the future, and keep training until you're able to run the whole 26 miles. Would you rather bounce back, or bounce forward?

Situations where you encounter adversity and trauma provide the richest learning experiences

Situations where you encounter adversity and trauma provide the richest learning experiences while also helping to develop resilience. Learning is the conduit through which failures can be turned into successes. The adaptability pillar can enhance the future success of individuals by encouraging them to actively think about negative experiences and learn from them by reframing those experiences as opportunities for adapting, learning and positive development. Learning from negative experiences promotes higher performance and positivity post-trauma, which is often supported by actively seeking feedback, and an area we'll delve into in the next coaching chapter.

A high-profile advocate of seeking feedback, Elon Musk has referenced his belief that maintaining a constant feedback loop, whereby you're constantly reflecting on what you've achieved and how you can make it even better, is one of the most important actions you can take to support peak performance and facilitate innovation.[7] More than just seeking feedback, though, Musk suggests questioning yourself[8] – being flexible in how you think about and tackle obstacles, adapting behaviour to create better results, and focusing on continuous improvement.[9]

There is perhaps no greater attribute that impacts the success of a business than adaptability. Take the well-known pivot the Starbucks business made after Howard Schultz visited Italy in 1983, a year after he joined Starbucks as a director of retail operations and marketing. Prior to Schultz's Italian adventure, Starbucks was a coffee business – it was all about the beans. The Starbucks store sold coffee beans, and Schultz had persuaded the owners to move to a model where coffee was brewed and served too. That iteration of Starbucks was, however, far from the bustling Starbucks coffee shops we see all over the world today.

In Milan, Schultz experienced first-hand how espresso bars could be part of a community, a place to gather. This is where Schultz came up with his vision of the 'third space' between home and work, somewhere people get to know each other, stop a while, and today even work. Mental agility – connecting dots between how coffee is consumed in Italy and applying that to a US market, and adapting the corporate strategy based on new information – allowed Schultz to shift the focus from just coffee to the space where that coffee is consumed. Schultz has since reflected that Starbucks was always a coffee business, but prior to adapting the vision, it was the wrong part of the business. Coffee is still at the core of what Starbucks does well, but the customer experience isn't just the coffee – it's every step of walking into a Starbucks store, ordering coffee, stopping a while and using that space.

Another key factor associated with adaptable resilience is learning how to fail, which is something Daniel Ek, the founder of Spotify, encourages – his motto is to fail faster than anyone else, and the company's unique organizational culture is designed for experimentation, learning and agility to continually optimize the way employees work. A barrier to building resilience is the stigma of failing; often, people are fearful of their credibility being tarnished if they try something new and it doesn't work out as planned. This fear can create a feeling of being stuck in a situation and unable to take action. In reality, real failure only exists when you fail to learn from the experience.

real failure only exists when you fail to learn from the experience

The speed at which we practise flexible thinking is important when it comes to mental agility. In order to adapt and evolve in a fast-paced world, we need to be able to challenge our own thinking, quickly. Practising a flexible mindset approach can result in finding opportunities to change, seeking out innovative new processes and taking action to respond to events rather than freezing or avoiding obstacles, all of which are factors associated with building resilience.

Positivity

There's strong evidence to support the idea that positivity and optimism are related to high levels of resilience, which are formed through the presence of positive emotions, and the ability to deal with negative emotions.[10] Positive emotions have in fact been shown to help with stress recovery. Research has shown that highly resilient people tend to display positive emotions, even when facing adversity or stress,[11] and those with positive expectations – which is a view that your future looks positive, and you'll fare better than is generally expected – have a lower risk of depressive symptoms and low mood when faced with adversity.[12]

As Martin Seligman pointed out in his book *Authentic Happiness*, the scale of optimism is vast, and some people are naturally more optimistic than others.[13] Optimism is, however, something that can be built, no matter where you are on the scale. If you imagine on a scale of one to ten, you're at the lower end – maybe a three – you may not realistically be able to boost your optimism to a ten (you also may not want to). But you don't need to be at the top end of the scale to start benefiting from the impact optimism can have on your life. You just need to push the dial a bit, maybe from a three to a five or six on the scale. This means optimism can be learned, much like resilience, which is reassuring to know when in the midst of dealing with challenges and uncertainty at work. You may not feel that your future is bright right now, or in general. But you can find ways to make small changes to strengthen your positivity pillar, some of which I'll share in the next coaching chapter.

Individuals tend to have a typical style when it comes to dealing with obstacles – which may be more or less negative.[14] Perhaps surprisingly, psychologists argue that the key to resilience is not putting an overly positive slant on every adverse scenario. Instead, the key is to be *flexible*, to think carefully about an experience before labelling it as good, bad or neutral, which is part of learning from negative experiences in order to build resilience.

Although being optimistic can be a positive tool in boosting resilience, it's important to focus on *realistic* optimism. Being overly optimistic can lead to blind hope, whereby you don't necessarily have a plan detailing how goals will be reached, rather you *hope* you'll achieve goals. Although it may seem this outlook could boost resilience, in fact, this approach is a common trap that can diminish resilience and increase stress. If you set targets and just will them into fruition, without the necessary action or a plan, you may not be in a position to reach those goals – and if that's the case, it can be a demoralizing and challenging place to be. The key to working on building optimism to enhance resilience is to be hopeful and to choose an optimistic approach, but also be mindful of your reality and be clear on what actions you need to take to give yourself the best shot of realizing goals. I often describe this as having your head and vision in the clouds, and one foot on the ground in reality.

Energy is also a big part of resilience, and in particular steering energy in a way that helps to build the psychological reserves required to deal with challenges. While the Dyson vacuum cleaner is now one of the most innovative and well-known cleaning devices around, there was a time when many people didn't believe in it. James Dyson reportedly created a massive 5,126 failed prototypes before he got the idea right, a test of his own optimism as he continued to work on his engineering innovation, believing he could find the right solution.[15]

Resilience can mean perseverance, but it also requires conscious and thoughtful energy management

Once Dyson had finalized his invention, he then struggled to convince a distributor in the UK to take a chance on something that pushed the boundaries of innovation so far.

Dyson instead went to Japan, where the product was a hit and won an industrial award. Rather than continue to pursue his strategic plan to find ways to work in the UK, he smartly steered his energy somewhere else – towards changing his strategy and reaching his goals in a different way. However, after getting a patent to sell in the US, manufacturers still didn't want to take it on. So, ten years after the Dyson vacuum was created, Dyson set up his own company to market the product and made it a huge success. Resilience can mean perseverance, but it also requires conscious and thoughtful energy management, and then an optimistic view of what can be achieved, grounded in a solid, and sometimes agile, plan.

Perspective

One thing psychology has taught us is how you view the world is how you experience the world. Two people can be in exactly the same situation but may experience it differently. Take a team being laid off in the workplace – for some this is catastrophic, for others it's an opportunity to try something new. Of course, personal circumstances will play a role in how a situation can affect you. If you're the sole provider for a family, it may be a more challenging experience than someone at the start of their career with no family responsibilities. But these practical factors are only part of how we experience situations. Take a recent coaching programme I was running where this exact scenario played out, and actually it was the new graduate who felt desperately overwhelmed at the prospect of losing their job, not the father of three children, who was the sole financial provider and had wanted to challenge himself to find a role in another industry for years but hadn't because of a fear of it not working out. Being laid off gave him the push to try to start his own business – he was focused on the opportunity that lay ahead, not the security he was losing.

Adjusting your perspective can at times require your thinking process to be challenged, particularly in difficult situations such as a project not playing out as you'd hoped, or project funding being pulled. This could seem like a failure. Or consider a new product or service you've been developing that just doesn't achieve your desired results. Reframing these experiences so you don't think of them as failures, but in fact as an important part of the learning process that will help you to progress and build tolerance for challenges and resilience in the future, is a positive approach to take. This will encourage you to push the boundaries of your abilities and venture into new experiences.

If you're a leader, and you want your team to be resilient when dealing with complex challenges and change, it's crucial that you consider your approach to failure. Ideally, you want to create a team environment that allows individuals to safely learn from failure, and a culture whereby feedback is freely given. If you're more naturally risk adverse, you may need to explore your tolerance for ambiguity and, at times, failure, to understand whether you're providing your team with the opportunity to put their problem-solving skills into practice, test new approaches and focus on innovation. Of course, risks need to be assessed, and it may not be possible to work in an environment where every new idea can be tested. Some risks are extremely high and have the potential to cause huge financial or reputational damage to the business, and it may not be appropriate to manage more than one or two projects that imply this level of risk across the team. Where it strategically makes sense, role-model and facilitate testing new approaches with your team – champion the successes and frame the failures as critical learning experiences.

The story of Herbert Hyman, the founder of The Coffee Bean & Tea Leaf, a small coffee and tea shop business in LA and Hollywood, is a perfect example of using a change in perspective to tackle adversity. When Starbucks threatened to put the company out of business by surrounding

Coffee Bean stores if Hyman didn't sell his business, contrary to an initial assessment of the situation, Hyman realized that having Starbucks surround his stores might not actually be a bad thing.[16] Instead of selling to the coffee giant, Hyman just let it do its thing – and realized that with a Starbucks next door, traffic to the area increased and sales soared. Starbucks boosted Hyman's sales so much that the smaller coffee shop began strategically targeting locations near the chain as a tactic and was able to expand instead of going out of business as Hyman was originally worried would happen. What was a huge commercial threat turned out to be the best thing that ever happened to Coffee Bean stores, according to Hyman. Not only did Hyman switch up his perspective and embrace the fact that his strategy may fail, he also accepted the situation, rather than fight it. Often, we focus on what we want to achieve, particularly in a performance-focused corporate world. But sometimes events unfold that we can't predict. The key to building resilience is taking control of your direction in that particular context, where you can, but also accepting what you can't change and mistakes you may make.

Mastery

Becoming a master at nurturing, replenishing and maintaining resilience requires a focus on three components: growth mindset, goals and flow. Often the need to build resilience is time-sensitive – you need to deal with a new challenge or a big change right now. This makes perfect sense, you want tools and strategies to help you in the moment, and that's often how we build knowledge – consider how many times you've Googled something you need help with in-the-moment over the last month. However, when I'm asked when is the best time to build resilience, I always respond: Before you need it. That's because if you start to build your resilience reservoir before your levels are depleted, you put yourself in a stronger position to deal with challenges (although the second-best time is right now, so read on if your resilience needs a boost today). Think of it as strategically planning for a future drought and building your resilience reserves in advance – this is what the mastery pillar of resilience helps you to do.

In 2003, Lego was struggling. Its sales had dropped 30 per cent and the business was reportedly £800 million in debt. That same year, the business promoted Jørgen Vig Knudstorp to CEO, who began a complete rebuild of the organization and its innovation practices, culminating in Lego becoming the world's most powerful brand in 2015 in what has been called the greatest turnaround in corporate history.[17] Vig Knudstorp identified that Lego had been over-innovating, trying to do too many things it didn't have any expertise in – such as clothing, theme parks and video games. Vig Knudstorp switched the focus towards leveraging Lego's core capabilities instead, observing how children *really* play and using that information to create new play experiences, using a low-risk, low-cost approach. This allows for mistakes to be made cheaply, prototypes to get to market at speed to be tested, and important learning opportunities. In the same ethos, Lego began to crowd-source ideas from customers, suppliers and partners to drive innovation, and to use digital tools to engage and connect with consumers.

It can be easy to assume a growth mindset means doing more or producing more – after all, if growth isn't about increasing size, what is it about? We'll dive into this topic in more detail in Chapter 6, but actually, when it comes to a growth mindset, it's about learning more and stretching the boundaries of abilities and knowledge. In the case of Lego, adopting a growth mindset of continuous development and learning actually resulted in reduced product lines and stripping back products to core offerings that had proven to be successful in the past. This coupled with strategic goal setting – being very specific about goals – which in the case of Lego was increasing profitability again, even if that meant letting go of some innovations – can create a powerful resilience combination that enables challenges to be overcome.

Everything the company has done in the years since Vig Knudstorp took the helm has been in line with the simplified strategy he laid out, and it's what has helped Lego to stay resilient and agile throughout the Covid-19 pandemic. For example, in 2020 executives saw that searches on Pinterest for children's schedules and stress relief were increasing week on week and they used this to create activity-related content for those stuck at home.

Research shows a high level of mastery improves resilience because it allows the individual to feel they are in control of the situation.[18] Reflecting on ways you have coped with adverse situations in the past may help you to feel capable and able to master skills to deal with future adversity, which can increase levels of resilience.

Another perhaps unlikely way to build mastery isn't to focus on resilience at all, but rather find your flow. This concept was devised by psychologist Mihaly Csikszentmihalyi, and refers to activities that are challenging, require skill and are enjoyable for the individual taking part.[19] Importantly, taking part in these activities helps to build psychological reserves, which has the benefit of boosting resilience. Different activities will create flow for different individuals – it may be something physical like running, hiking or yoga, or something that takes concentration, such as playing chess or solving puzzles. Or it could be a new skill you're developing, such as cooking, mechanics or learning a language. If you've ever taken part in an activity that you enjoy, that stretches your abilities, with the potential for you to develop and get better, and you've been so absorbed in the activity you've lost track of time – you may be in flow. When you're in flow you also have a clear understanding of what you want to achieve – your goal.

Mastering your resilience journey takes time and focus. The pay-off is, however, high. You may not know what challenges are coming your way at work, but if you can take control of your resilience journey and boost your resilience reserves, you put yourself in the best position possible to overcome future adversity.

Stamina

When Sheryl Sandberg lost her husband Dave Goldberg, she had to learn a lot about resilience – the most tragic way. Sandberg is well known as the Chief Operating

Officer at Facebook. In *Option B*, the book she wrote with Wharton Professor of Psychology Adam Grant, she discusses the ideas of collective resilience and the importance of coming together as a community and supporting one another, even if you can't be physically together.[20] This is a powerful reminder of how support is such an important part of building resilience.

A study of fire fighters found that higher levels of social support related to enhanced resilience and improved health – indicating Sandberg's concept of collective resilience is also applicable in various contexts within the workplace.[21] In fact, support was one of the key factors identified as a critical construct of resilience in a review of the individual factors that together create the construct of resilience.[22] For leaders, putting structures in place to promote socially supportive environments – whether that be peer, managerial or personal support – is one of the most simple and effective ways to create a culture of resilience and enhance team resilience overall.

Resilience stamina is about nurturing resilience over the long term. Often, it's assumed that the best way to create resilience is to avoid adversity, but research has found this to be inaccurate. Moderate exposure to adversity has in fact been found to enhance resilience and protect against not only current adversity, but future trauma also.[23] If you want to build resilience, you need a certain amount of pressure, so you can learn how to deal with the situation effectively and build confidence in your ability to tackle future challenges. If you never experience challenges, you have no way of building your resilience. Equally, too much pressure can deplete your resilience reserves. The key is being very conscious about your resilience-building strategy when it's in your control, finding ways to push outside of your comfort zone and embracing pressure and challenge. This will allow you to function at peak performance, operating at peak levels without being adversely affected by high levels of stress.

Small shifts, big impact

The key to building resilience at work is to focus on small changes over the long term. The nature of building resilience requires exposure to challenges, learning from experience and figuring out what helps you to nurture your resilience in different situations. The truth is these can be very simple steps, but you can't fast-track the process or take shortcuts. This is why building resilience is a mindset – a way of thinking and processing information – and to build resilience over the long term, you need to build a resilient way of thinking into everyday life.

It's important to remember resilience fluctuates over time and across contexts. You may find a resilience strategy that works for you in particular situations, perhaps when juggling multiple sources of pressure in your personal and working life, but the same strategies may not be so helpful when dealing with one huge challenge, such as being made redundant. Equally, we change over time. How you deal with adversity today may not be the way you would have dealt with obstacles years ago. It's so important to regularly reflect on your resilience journey, test out strategies and approaches, learn to identify your stress triggers and warning signals, and keep working on tweaking your resilience strategy in a way that works for you – one small step at a time. In the next coaching chapter, we'll explore exercises and strategies to help with this.

Resilience is effectively about how we adapt to and cope with change. At a corporate or organizational level, resilience can be improved by studying and profiling the elasticity of an organization – such as understanding the factors that allow an organization to bounce forward during times of change, and factors that are less adaptable and elastic, and present barriers to change.[24] This process of resilience profiling can be applied to personal resilience also by analysing the factors that affect your ability to be agile and flexible in responding to obstacles and using that information to pre-plan strategy and tactics for dealing with change. This way, focusing on resilience becomes proactive rather than reactionary.

Resilience isn't about enduring adversity. Rather, nurturing resilience is about recovery and strengthening your ability to deal with challenges in the future by deploying strategies to keep moving through obstacles, without getting stuck. Sometimes this requires action, and at other times it requires rest and recovery, as we'll explore in the next chapter.

CHAPTER 03

Coaching: Bouncing forward

In this first of the coaching chapters, we'll explore coaching tools, techniques and strategies that have been designed to help you build your resilience.

Building your resilience reserves is your personal insurance policy, providing you with the confidence to know you can overcome the challenges that come your way in the future. The end-goal when building resilience isn't to be resilient, because as counter-intuitive as this may sound, the goal of being resilient is something you may never achieve. Let me explain why.

Resilience is dynamic – it changes over time depending on what's going on *within you* – factors such as personality, mood, attitude, beliefs can impact your resilience. You may have periods of time where your mood is lower than normal, and that can affect how you feel about the challenges you face. On the flip side, you may have periods of time where you feel elated, and that makes you feel like you can face any adversity with ease. These factors are changeable and sometimes unpredictable.

Your resilience will also change depending on what's going on *around you* – consider factors such as the amount of pressure you're dealing with at one point in time, how many challenges you're navigating throughout all areas of your life, or the support you have around you. If you're under intense pressure or you have multiple challenges going on in different areas of your life, you may find it difficult to navigate obstacles. And the reverse could occur; one big challenge may not throw you off course if you're not feeling overwhelmed by pressure. Imagine you have a strong support system – that may positively impact your resilience, and people within that support system may help you to tackle challenges. At the opposite end of the scale, a lack of support can make adversity seem impossible to deal with.

The point is, your resilience reserves will go up and down. Remember the analogy of a reservoir – sometimes your levels will be high, and at other times you may experience a resilience drought. So, if your goal is to be resilient all of the time, you could be setting yourself up for a fall, because there are so many factors at play that impact your resilience. The problem with aiming for resilience as the ultimate end-goal is you may feel like you've failed when that isn't achievable, but in reality you may not have been able to control that outcome.

I recommend a more achievable goal of aiming to build your resilience toolkit, rather than trying to be resilient all the time. This goal can be measured, as you can calculate the resilience boosting techniques you've learned and tested. This also shifts the focus from the outcome of resilience – which you can't always control – towards the actions you can take to build your resilience reserves – which is in your control. If you can focus on building your resilience toolkit before you face challenges, you'll have techniques and strategies ready to use should adversity hit. Equally, if you're facing challenges right now, it's the perfect time to start testing coaching tools to determine what makes a difference for you.

Before I dive into resilience-enhancing strategies, it's important to reiterate we're all individuals. Some strategies will work for you, others you may want to test but later decide they don't need to be in your resilience-building toolkit right now. You may also find some techniques work for where you are in your life right now, and others may work when you face different challenges or situations in the future. In this coaching chapter I'll detail evidence-based exercises and strategies I use when coaching clients to support resilience. This is your manual to help you thrive at work today and in the future. Use the exercises you need right now, and come back to these ideas as and when needed.

Building your six pillars of resilience

We'll focus on the six pillars of resilience discussed in Chapter 2:

1 Confidence
2 Adaptability
3 Positivity
4 Perspective
5 Mastery
6 Stamina

Confidence

The more confident you are, the more likely it is that you'll be able to deal with challenges effectively and take bold steps to overcome roadblocks that threaten to knock you off course. Your confidence will encourage you to thrive and move closer to achieving the goals that are important to you.

Building confidence in the context of resilience is about believing in your own ability to take action when you face adversity and finding answers when an obstacle strikes. It isn't about having all the answers ready or feeling confident in every new situation you step into. Rather, it's having confidence *in yourself* and feeling that you can find the answers, potentially with the help of others or other resources.

Here's an exercise you can try to boost your self-belief and focus on action steps that are in your control.

◉ CONFIDENCE WEEKLY REFLECTION EXERCISE
Take some time this week to reflect on challenges and achievements. In particular, focus on what was in your control when you were dealing with challenges, and what was out of your control. You might also want to consider

where you were focusing your energy – on the part of the situation you could or couldn't control? Often, we can spend much of our time ruminating over parts of a challenge we can't change, but to build resilience we need to switch that to focus on what we can change. You can use the template in Table 3.1 to support you in this exercise.

For example, you may have found out that a project you've been working on has had the budget cut and all progress you've made over the past months working on this may feel wasted. I've worked with many clients in this situation, and I've faced it myself. It's disappointing, perhaps even devastating.

But could you change your thinking to consider what you can control? Could you salvage relationships with key stakeholders to deliver the news personally? This may support you in building strong relationships and a network for the future. Can you repurpose any of the outputs you created? Or save some of the work for potential future projects? Can you focus on what you learned in the process of managing the project? At times this learning can feel pointless, but learning is rarely obsolete; you will carry that new knowledge with you in your career.

Also consider your achievements, however small they may seem. All too often we forget small wins along the way and focus on parts of our working life that didn't go to plan. You can rectify this by reflecting on small achievements and celebrating along the way, which is an important process as this primes your thoughts towards achievements, which over time can make achieving goals part of your everyday life (building your confidence in the process). Take some time to ponder how you would achieve your goals again – would you do this in the same way? If so, acknowledging this sends a message to your sub-conscious mind – you can be confident in finding ways to achieve your goals. You may also identify other ways you would achieve the same goal, perhaps tweaking your approach slightly. Again, this is brilliant – you're learning and adapting your approach which can build your belief in your ability to deal with challenges over time.

Finally, consider the extent to which you believe you can navigate challenges that come your way, and what you could do to enhance this belief in your ability to overcome obstacles. Part of being confident is believing you have control over your direction in life and the outcomes you achieve – it's the opposite of feeling life is happening *to* you, but rather you can direct your life.

Adaptability

The world of work will be continually evolving, that isn't set to change. Today at work we have no choice but to be adaptable, responsive and agile. When building resilience, adaptability can play to your advantage – you may not be able to change the scenario you find yourself in, but you can change your response to the situation. Being conscious of how you think about events and managing the process will help you to cope with challenges in new and effective ways and reduce your stress levels in tough situations.

◎ FLEXIBLE THINKING EXERCISE
Flexible thinking is a powerful tool at your disposal that can help you to become more adaptable, and in the process

TABLE 3.1   Confidence weekly reflection template

Challenges faced this week	Things I could control
1	●
	●
	●
2	**Things I couldn't control**
	●
3	●
	●

Achievements this week	How would I achieve these things again?
1	●
2	●
3	●

Belief in my ability to deal with challenges that come my way – where am I on this scale?	What could I do to enhance my belief in my ability to navigate challenges?
	●
	●
	●

Low   Medium   High

build your resilience. The patterns of thinking you use day-to-day can be helpful in preventing you from becoming overwhelmed by the sheer amount of information your brain is processing – you need these cognitive shortcuts. It would be challenging if you had to assess every new situation without relying on previous context to make a quick decision. For example, you don't spend hours in the supermarket researching what kind of pasta to buy – you rely on information about products you've tried and tested before.

Although useful, this pattern thinking can also be our downfall at times, as we can find ourselves in a rut. Have you ever found yourself in a situation where you expect the worse to happen? Or you expect to have a challenging conversation? This can be caused by prior experience priming you when you enter similar situations, or you may have got used to thinking in this way, which causes a bias towards negativity when entering new situations.

One of the common ways we can limit ourselves when it comes to building resilience is by allowing permanent negative thoughts to continue over time. Let me explain what I mean by this. When you make a mistake, do you ever think to yourself, 'I *always* get this wrong', or 'I *never* get it right when trying new things'? In these instances, you're using fixed, permanent statements – words such as 'always' and 'never', and they're being used to imply a negative outcome. So much of this thinking is done subconsciously, it's hard to detect at times.

Permanent statements aren't always an issue. Imagine if you flipped the statements above to 'I *never* look at experiences as getting it wrong, I *always* learn something' or 'I *always* get it right when I try new things'. The issue with permanent statements is when they imply negative outcomes. You can challenge yourself to consciously catch these thoughts in your head, and replace either the permanent statement, using words such as 'sometimes' or 'on this occasion'. So, the thoughts might change like this:

I *always* get it wrong	→	*Sometimes* it takes me a few attempts get it right
I *never* get it right	→	*Today* I didn't find the right solution

When you find yourself using permanent negative statements, replace the permanence focus, or alter the outcome so it's not negative, such as:

I got it wrong	→	I'm learning
(negative outcome)		(positive outcome)

Changing how you think about a situation can change how you behave. Imagine you have a meeting at work, and you feel like you're walking into a hostile environment where you need to challenge a colleague who isn't performing – how do you think these thoughts might affect your behaviour going into the meeting? If you change that to expecting to talk to your colleague and find a collaborative solution together, how do you think your behaviour may change? Often, what we expect to happen in a situation heavily influences how the interaction plays out. If you're mindful of this, you can alter how you approach situations to result in a better outcome.

Positivity

In order to navigate change and choose your direction to move forward, you need an objective understanding of where you are now. When it comes to building the positivity pillar of resilience, optimism is important, but ultimately it's *realistic* optimism that's the crucial factor in building resilience. This is because blind hope or wishing for a better future can be detrimental to psychological health when plans don't work out. Consider someone starting a business and hoping to attract new clients but with no plan for how to make this happen. That could create a psychological impact such as causing stress or anxiety. Optimism has huge benefits for performance and can reduce feelings of sadness, depression and anxiety, but you also need an action plan to provide you with the best shot of reaching goals. It's important to remember when you're setting big goals to give yourself time to reach them, and to have a clear plan of action. It's often said we overestimate what we can achieve in a year, and underestimate what we can achieve in five years.

Although some of us are more naturally optimistic than others, everyone can move along the scale of optimism (Table 3.2). You may find yourself at the lower end of the optimism scale naturally, perhaps at a two. You can learn to shift up the scale, maybe towards a five. Equally, you may be at a seven on the scale, and you can move your levels to a nine or ten. It isn't about making drastic changes, it's about small shifts that over time help you to see the world with a more optimistic outlook.

TABLE 3.2   Optimism scale

0   5   10

◎ GRATITUDE EXERCISE

One of the most effective and simple ways to build optimism is to practise gratitude. When navigating an unpredictable and complex environment at work, thinking about the challenges you face can become all-consuming. A tell-tale sign of this can be trouble sleeping or switching off, or relationships feeling strained. Although the challenges you face can't always be removed, you do have the power to choose how you view the world. This isn't about replacing negative thoughts and emotions with positivity – partly because this isn't possible, and partly because that may not be a healthy coping mechanism (it can put you in 'blind hope' territory). You can, however, focus on what is going well in your life *as well as* what isn't so desirable, providing a more balanced view of your life as a whole.

Take a few moments every morning or evening to update a journal, noting at least three things you feel grateful for. These could be small things such as a catch up with a friend, a walk in the sunshine, a good coffee or a bedtime story with a child. Or they could be large things, such as getting the go-ahead on a project, receiving some good health news, reaching a big goal you set yourself. Practising gratitude can reset your thinking and remove the focus from what's not going so well to areas of your life that are going well. Over time this can boost optimism and help you to view challenges through a more positive lens, empowering you to feel that you can tackle problems, or place your focus on positive aspects of your life, which can help to build resilience.

Perspective

One of the key concepts to grasp when building resilience is the idea that you have a perspective – a way of viewing the world – that's different to how others see the world; and that it is one *possible* way of viewing situations, not necessarily the *only* correct way. If you can develop the ability to see situations from alternative points of view, this will enable you to be open to new ideas and creatively respond to obstacles.

◎ DETECTING ROOT CAUSE EXERCISE

Often it can be helpful to identify the root cause of your responses. You may have a colleague who you find particularly challenging to work with because they block your progress – maybe they don't respond with information you need, or they always seem to have a comment that suggests your project plan won't work.

Even though it may seem these interactions would bother everyone, they wouldn't. They bother you because of how you think about the situation. Yes, it's annoying that you feel like your work process is being hindered, but what is it that really bothers you? You can start to identify this by asking yourself the question 'Why?' repeatedly.

Here's an example of how you can start to figure out what's really bothering you:

I'm annoyed Sarah hasn't provided me with the sales
figures again, so I'll have to produce my report
at the last minute, again.

↓

Why is this annoying?

↓

Because it's disrespectful.

↓

Why is this disrespectful?

↓

Because it makes me feel that my value is undermined.

↓

Why does that feel bad?

↓

I've worked hard to prove my value and
it hasn't always been noticed before.

↓

Why is your value being noticed important?

↓

I need recognition to be able to progress on my career,
and provide a good life for my family.

The idea is you keep asking yourself 'why' questions until you get to a deeper reason of why you're upset with a situation or struggling to deal with challenges effectively. Once you have this insight, you can work with the knowledge you have about how you perceive the situation.

In this example, you may feel that your colleague is disrespectful, but that's not what is really going on.

Underneath it all, you have a need for recognition because you believe that is the key to supporting your family. Sarah, your colleague, doesn't know this though – it's not part of her perspective in this situation.

So, you have two choices to deal with this challenge. You can make Sarah aware of your perspective and ask her to change her behaviour, or you can change how you view this situation and decide this one interaction does not define your value at work, and you will focus on demonstrating your value in other ways. This won't make the situation less irritating, but it could reduce the intense emotions you feel every time you encounter the situation. You also have the option of turning the experience into learning for the future.

There is no right way to respond here – it depends on your personal situation and what you would like to achieve. The point is, you're working to understand your own perspective, and the reasons that you experience challenges in the way you do. If there's something about a situation you want to change, getting clear on your thought process and the impact that it has on how you feel and behave can be a powerful step in adjusting how you deal with challenges.

The next time you face a challenge you're struggling to get past, take some time to figure out the root cause of what's going on. Keep asking yourself 'why' questions until you feel that you've got to the bottom layer – your deep beliefs. Then you need to decide what action to take, and you have two options:

1 Change something about the situation – for example this could be discussing your perspective with others or

changing your behaviour (it's important to remember you can't necessarily change other people's thoughts or behaviours – so don't focus on this).

2 Find a way to accept the situation as you have no control over it, or accept when you've made a mistake.

Once you're clear on why you view the world in the way you do, you can start to work on understanding the perspectives of others – which is something we'll cover in Chapter 9, when we discuss emotional intelligence coaching.

Mastery

Continually focusing on growing and nurturing your resilience is an important part of mastering your resilience journey. Your resilience reserves will fluctuate over time, but by placing your attention on resilience in your day-to-day life, you will over time help to build psychological tools to boost your resilience when you feel depleted. Finding ways to boost your resilience is essential if you want to be able to effectively deal with the challenges you face today, and potential challenges you'll face in the future. One of the ways to do this it to find your 'flow'.

Psychologist Mihaly Csikszentmihalyi coined the term 'flow' in the 1990s in his revolutionary book *Flow*.[1] Finding and focusing on your flow can be a powerful tool to build your resilience over the long term. When you're in a state of flow, you're absorbed in an activity that you enjoy, but also find challenging. These activities push your skill boundaries, you can always get slightly better with practice. When you're taking part in these activities, you're not thinking about anything else. In fact, time often feels like it's standing still, and you can lose hours absorbed in what you're doing.

For some people, flow could be physical activities such as hiking, golf, building Lego or designing model aeroplanes. For others it could be learning a cognitive skill such as a new language or a musical instrument. For some it could be problem solving, such as coding or working out formulas in a spreadsheet. Flow is an enjoyable (if at times challenging) experience, and these activities can also re-energize you and recharge your energy levels when obstacles you've been dealing with have left them depleted. As you progress in stretching your skills and abilities in the activities that provide flow for you, you may also find your confidence builds – supporting your belief in your ability to navigate uncertainty.

You may have an idea about the activities that create flow and recharge you, or you may want to take some time to focus on this. Here's an exercise that can help.

◎ FINDING FLOW EXERCISE

Take some time to reflect on activities that create a sense of flow for you. These activities will:

- stretch your ability
- help you to develop skills or get better at something
- require you to focus to the extent that you lose track of time
- stop you from thinking about anything else

Over the next couple of weeks, note what kinds of activities do this for you by using the template in Table 3.3.

TABLE 3.3   Identifying flow template

Activities that create flow for me	Things I enjoy about these activities

How can I build more of these challenges into my week?

1

2

3

Once you're clear on the activities that create a sense of flow for you, consider how you can build these into your week to act as a moment to re-charge, and to switch your focus away from thinking about challenges you're currently dealing with, towards focusing on the activity you're taking part in. Your flow activities could be work-related, or you may find they're not. If hiking creates a sense of flow, you could perhaps make a regular date to do this at lunchtime, in the evening or at weekends.

It's important to remember re-charging and rest are crucial factors that support resilience. It's not just about pushing through with grit and perseverance when you face obstacles. If you're serious about building your resilience so challenges don't become overwhelming, dedicating time to flow activities every week may become a non-negotiable activity for you.

Stamina

Increasing your resilience stamina will enable you to build the momentum required to 'bounce forward' when you hit a roadblock. Understanding and accepting that you will get knocked off-course throughout your career journey, and that your stamina is the key to keep you moving, will help you to learn from experiences and achieve more in the future.

Navigating uncertainty and complex working environments doesn't involve finding ways to minimize challenges, as you won't always have control over this. Your focus needs to be on equipping yourself to deal with challenges effectively. There is so much about the working world and the future of work that's unknown that you can't predict the challenges you'll face in the future. What you can predict is whether you'll have the psychological tools to deal with new challenges that occur, and the only way you can guarantee this is by practising exercises that will support you in building your resilience.

It's important to build a structure around you that supports resilience. This could include a process whereby you regularly include resilience-boosting activities in your week, such as exercise, rest, time in nature, mindfulness, connecting with people important to you. It could also include being conscious of building a strong support system around you – which is one of the most critical and yet under-utilized resilience-building strategies.

◎ BUILDING A BOARD OF SUPPORTERS EXERCISE

Take some time to map out your support structure. Think about who you rely on for support and how that person helps you. You more than likely find you turn to different people for various kind of support – some people may have specific experiences or a perspective they can share with you, others may be great at listening, some people may offer honest advice.

Consider how you would create a board of directors, or in this case a board of supporters, who help to guide you when you experience challenging periods. The idea is you have so many supporter seats available on your board, and you want different kinds of people to offer support in different situations. The template in Table 3.4 can guide you through this exercise.

Once you map out your board of supporters, you may find you have seats available where you'd benefit from more support. Perhaps you have a supportive family network, but you could do with a workplace mentor to offer advice and experience. Or perhaps you have a strong support system at work, but you would benefit from more people around you outside of work to help you deal with adversity. When you're clear on where you need more support, you can seek out people to help with that – maybe a coach, mentor or support group.

TABLE 3.4   Board of supporters template

Who I rely on for support	How these people help me
⊛	⊛
⊛	⊛
⊛	⊛
⊛	⊛
⊛	⊛
⊛	⊛
⊛	⊛

People I provide support for	Areas where I'd like more support
⊛	⊛
⊛	
⊛	⊛
⊛	
⊛	⊛
⊛	
⊛	⊛

Also consider who you offer support to. Helping others can be altruistic and can change your focus from considering the help you need from others to get past obstacles, towards considering the skills and attributes you can share with others to overcome challenges. This can provide a sense of meaning and connection, something we'll touch on in more detail in Chapter 10.

Building resilience for the long term

Checking in with yourself regularly to reflect on where your resilience levels are can help you to understand patterns in your resilience. You might start to identify whether you find a particular situation, person or period challenging, and that impacts your resilience. Or you may be experiencing a long period of uncertainty that requires you to draw deeply on your resilience reserves. The key point here is awareness – understanding where you are on your resilience path, and the reasons why.

Resilience can't be an effective or healthy end goal. Psychological resilience isn't static; it will change over time. You'll have experiences where your resilience levels feel higher than normal, and others where those levels feel lower. If you're chasing the feeling of high levels of resilience, you will at times find yourself disappointed. A more effective approach to building resilience is focusing on what you can control – learning tools and strategies that you can access and utilize when you need them. I've used exercises in this chapter to help you do just that.

These exercises aren't the complete toolbox for building resilience, they are the strategies I use most frequently with clients who want to learn how to thrive in uncertainty. You can access more resilience strategies on my website (see page 1). It's important to understand resilience is *part* of your toolkit when it comes to navigating challenges, change and uncertainty; in the next chapter we'll delve into how cognitive flexibility can be used as a tool to help you to thrive at work.

CHAPTER 04

Cognitive flexibility

At the heart of it, your mindset is a set of beliefs and thoughts that affect how you behave. So, when it comes to nurturing a mindset for success, understanding how you think and process information is important. Once you understand your thinking process, you can focus on tweaking it to achieve a better outcome for you – whether that be improving performance, wellbeing or motivation. The first step is understanding your current thinking patterns, the next step is choosing how to process information. As you'll see later in this chapter, sometimes you may want to tweak your thinking and behaviour, at other times you might prefer to take the approach where you accept your thoughts and continue to keep moving forward at the same time. I'll explain how both approaches work, and you can make the choice about how to set up your mindset for success. One thing is for certain – it will be a very personal and individual process.

When I was an undergraduate student studying psychology for the first time, I had a career-defining moment in a lecture. I learned that *everyone* on the planet thinks differently and responds to events in their own unique way. This might sound like a simple and obvious statement, but that realization blew my mind. I felt like everything I thought I had known about how humans think and behave was shattered. It was a very uncomfortable moment – how could I be a psychologist and help people to understand their thinking patterns, enhance performance, improve relationships and be happier if I couldn't understand how every human thinks? Because, as I was learning, it's impossible to understand the thought process of every person you encounter. And how could I help people to find solutions to improve their lives, when there are no definitive ways of doing this? And while we're at it, how could I use scientific research to help people, when almost every theory presented had an equally plausible counter-theory?

I hadn't realized before that moment, but I had assumed that in my psychology lectures I would learn the 'right' way of thinking and processing information. And if not the correct way, at least the most effective. I would have happily taken even just a handful of absolute, tried and tested, one-hundred-per-cent effective techniques to work with. What I learned instead is there are a whole host of considerations that can impact how we think and behave.

Thinking and responding

When it comes to understanding how we think and process information, there are individual neurobiological factors to consider – everyone's nervous system (including the brain) functions in a different way. Sure, there are patterns, but why, for example, do some people suffer with seasonal affective disorder and experience lower moods in winter months, while others don't? Why is it that some people can consume caffeine late into the evening with no adverse impact on their sleep, while others can't consume any caffeine at all if they want to sleep well? Our nervous systems perform differently.

So how does this affect how we think, feel and behave? Well, if your nervous system works in a way that makes you more likely to experience depression, whether that be in darker months or in general, that's going to create a filter through which you view and experience events around you. If your sleep patterns aren't the most pro-ductive, and you're less rested than you could be, or normally are, this will most likely have a detrimental impact on how you approach challenges and how you process information. In short, biological factors that impact how our brains function can affect how we think and behave – our mindset. As any new parent or insomnia sufferer can attest to, sleep deprivation can at times make minor challenges feel like huge obstacles that can't always be overcome, and yet, once feeling rested again, thoughts about challenges can become more positive. As this example illustrates, neurobiological factors can affect our thinking process.

How we respond to events isn't all biology, however. There are also psychological factors such as attitude, motivation and personality to consider. Whereas neurological factors are influenced by chemical reactions in the brain, psychological factors have an impact on how we process information about the world around us and patterns that affect how we interact with others and the world.

When it comes to biological factors, the chemical effects can be measured by the presence or lack of chemical compounds in our body, such as neurotransmitters (e.g., dopamine and serotonin) and hormones (e.g., cortisol and adrenaline). Psychological factors are different, they're more about patterns of thinking, which it can take time and effort to decode and understand.

You've more than likely come across the nature or nurture debate, and the jury is out as to whether we're born with a personality type, and whether our environment shapes personality, and equally whether personality is fixed or changes over time. Regardless, your personality can affect how you process information. Although personality testing is a somewhat contentious issue within the psychologist community, the 'big five' is one of the most widely recognized measurements of personality and focuses on the traits of extraversion, openness to new experiences, conscientiousness, agreeableness and neuroticism – and the opposite ends of each scale (such as introversion being the opposite of extraversion).[1] Imagine you're high on the openness scale – the chances are you're going to approach new situations in a more open-minded and relaxed way than someone who is low on the scale, and the opposite may be true for those who are low on the openness scale

– new challenges may feel overwhelming. How you view the situation will in turn impact how you feel about the situation – either positively or negatively.

There are also other factors that affect how we think and process information. Experience shapes our view of the world. If you've faced challenges in the past and found resources either within yourself or external to you to overcome this adversity, when you face similar challenges in the future you may feel more confident in navigating obstacles compared to someone who hasn't had the same experience as you. This is partly how resilience is built over time. Other considerations are context and environment. You may be delivered the best piece of news you've had in a while, but if you're in a physical or psychological situation that doesn't make you happy you may not feel particularly elated. And, equally, if the environment around you is positive, you may feel more optimistic in how you approach challenging news, feeling like you can tackle any obstacles that are thrown your way.

Nurturing a mindset for success

How we process information is messy, complicated and dynamic. Which means when it comes to responding to events, we need a toolkit of different strategies and approaches that can be used in different ways – depending on your personality, biology, experience and the context you're in. We need to be mentally agile to manage how we feel and think about situations, and how we respond.

As I started out in my occupational psychology career, the hot topic was cognitive behavioural therapy (CBT) and helping people to reframe the way they see the world and perceive events, in order to manage emotions and ultimately change behaviour to achieve better results. This is a very handy approach to have in your toolkit, and I'll delve into it in more detail later in this chapter. Research then progressed to a focus on a new wave of psychotherapy: acceptance and commitment therapy (ACT). The gist of this approach is not to focus on eliminating difficult feelings, but rather use tools such as mindfulness to keep moving forward towards a valuable goal, even when the going gets tough. I will discuss this more later in this chapter, but for now it's interesting to explore the contrast between *changing* how you view the world and how you feel about events, versus *accepting* your feelings and finding ways to keep moving forward. Rather than championing one mindset approach over another, could there be a way to use both interchangeably in different contexts to help navigate change?

Rather than championing one mindset approach over another, could there be a way to use both interchangeably?

The adaptable thinking style

When it comes to coaching approaches that focus on thinking styles, understanding emotions, navigating feelings and applying behaviour, I'm very reluctant to focus on one type of solution. There is no one 'best' way to coach ourselves and others through challenges. Rather, there are a variety of ways you can use to reach the desired results. Sometimes one approach might work. In other situations, a completely different technique might be more effective, or comfortable, or preferable. I believe in giving people options when it comes to learning how to coach themselves. Even if I were convinced there was only one way to deal with challenges, I don't have an insight into your unique challenges, the situation you're in, how you respond to events, your history, your personality, your biology, so it wouldn't be effective to provide one universal solution that works for everyone.

In a coaching relationship some of this information will unfold, but it's not a coach's job to 'diagnose' someone and provide the solution. Rather, coaches help individuals understand more about themselves, the situation and possible approaches they can take to move forward. It's my job to support the people I coach as they test new approaches to dealing with challenges, reflect on the experience to figure out which strategies work better than others, and plan how to hone these techniques to create positive outcomes in the future.

The truth of the matter is, how our minds work is always evolving. We have the potential to be forever growing, learning and developing. So, when it comes to thriving in uncertainty, it's important to have a toolkit that includes a variety of strategies, tools and practices you can use to navigate change. And, ideally, you should add to this toolkit over time – there is always more to learn about yourself and the world around you that will shape how you respond to situations. The coaching chapters in this book have been included to help you build out your toolbox.

Switching perspectives

When Michael Jordan was a teenager, he didn't make his high school varsity basketball team because his coach told him he wasn't tall enough to play. This moment had a profound impact on him, and he has spoken about how crushed he was at the disappointment, and how he was ready to give up. However, his mother advised him to prove to the coach he had made a mistake and be the best player he could be. Jordan did just that, and decided to leave the disappointment behind, took accountability, and focused on the actions he could take to create the results he wanted by improving his performance. This is a lesson that helped drive Jordan's subsequent success as an athlete.

This example of reframing a negative situation into an opportunity is a key component of the cognitive behavioural coaching method, which is based on one of the psychotherapy methods I mentioned earlier – cognitive behavioural therapy. At the heart of this coaching method is understanding your view of the world and how that impacts feelings and emotions, and ultimately behaviour. Michael Neenan and Windy Dryden were the pioneers of this coaching method, and in their book *Life Coaching* they break down the concept using a five-stage model to reframe challenges and take steps to change the way we think about difficult situations.[2]

Often, when we consider a situation that hasn't gone well, we attribute the negative situation to something outside of ourselves – another person, or an event that occurred. I always use the example of feeling angry in the car – why is it that sometimes the behaviour of other drivers can leave you feeling stressed and angry, and at other times you can shrug it off as a mild annoyance? If the situation of dealing with inconsiderate drivers caused your stress, surely you would feel that same way every time you face one of these drivers? If I were to ask you in this situation what was causing your stress, you would most likely attribute the cause of that feeling to the behaviour of inconsiderate drivers. But the reality of the situation is how you think about the event plays a part in how you feel, and how you respond.

how you think about the event plays a part in how you feel, and how you respond

Using the ABCDE coaching model

How does this play out in the real world? Take the example of Michael Jordan being disappointed about not making his high school basketball team. An understandable response would be to blame the coach and be angry at the decision, becoming despondent in the process. But this isn't what happened. Rather, Jordan *chose* to view the situation differently. He may have been disappointed, he may have even felt angry, but Jordan chose his behaviour and response – he chose to work hard to prove his coach wrong.

The ABCDE model plays out in the following way:

A = *activating event* – the situation that unfolds. In this case, the coach told Jordan he didn't make the team.

B = *beliefs about the situation* – in this case Jordan believed he could prove the coach wrong.

C = consequences – so Jordan kept pushing forward and trying until he made the team.

Imagine this had gone a different way, and after the coach advised Jordan that he hadn't made the team (activating event) Jordan believed it was unfair but there was nothing he could do about the situation (beliefs). He may have given up trying to be the best basketball player he could be (the consequence). It's clear to see how beliefs and thoughts about a situation can impact behaviour, which will then have a consequence – either positive or negative.

Had Jordan found himself on a path where he had started to give up, it wouldn't have necessarily been the end of the road. In this coaching model you can learn to disrupt your beliefs and replace them with thoughts that can create a different outcome. So, for a young basketball player that had started to give up, they could learn to replace thoughts of:

'It's no use – there's nothing I can do to change this decision.'

with:

'I'm going to keep working to prove the coach wrong.'

This new way of thinking changes the thinking process and in this coaching model plays out like this:

D = disrupting thought – 'I'm going to keep working to prove the coach wrong.'

E = effective new approach – in this case, creating a plan to keep progressing and find ways to showcase progress and prove competence.

Consider how this applies to you in your working life. When you face an obstacle, challenge, or uncertainty, how often do you take the time to consider how your thoughts about the situation impact your behaviour? Perhaps you've been in a situation where you've been told your job is at risk and you've behaved in a way that isn't helpful – damaging relationships with colleagues or giving up and not focusing on quality delivery at work. Although these might be understandable reactions, they may not aid your future career development as strained relationships can be hard to repair and if you're not making progress at work it might be tricky to get a good reference later, or you may be less likely to get hired in the future if the hiring manager turns out to be someone you worked with in the role where your focus on quality delivery diminished.

Are there places in your life where you would benefit from disrupting your current thinking process? Maybe you've been thinking about a challenge, a colleague or a situation in a way that's holding you back. If this is the case, how else could you think about the situation to create a better outcome for you?

Accepting challenges

Learning how to change the way you think about challenging situations by disrupting and replacing your thoughts to serve you better is a strategy that has proved successful in dealing with change and uncertainty at work. Another method that has been proven to be just as effective (or even more effective in some situations) is acceptance and commitment therapy, which is a mindfulness-based behavioural technique.[3] Its aim is to focus on creating meaning in life, while accepting that pain is an inevitable part of life for all of us. The difference here when compared to cognitive behavioural coaching is with ACT there is no focus on changing your thoughts. Rather, you accept your thoughts and appreciate they're not representative of you as a person. Your thoughts are ways of processing information that you're experiencing currently, and they will pass and change. Both situations will play out differently, and there is no one 'right' mindset – it's more about choosing how to respond in different circumstances.

Part of the process of using ACT is to become clear on what your values are. Your core values are the things in life that are the most important to you, the principles or beliefs that you attach most meaning to. When you clearly understand what your core values are, they can act as your compass, providing a sense of direction and meaning. This makes you less likely to be thrown off course by events and obstacles; if you know where you're going, you can try to find a route to get there. Once you have this clarity, you can take mindful and conscious steps towards a meaningful life – which you can't necessarily do without staying true to your values.

When you clearly understand what your core values are, they can act as your compass

A renowned billionaire with her own television channel in the USA, Oprah Winfrey started her career at a small TV station in Tennessee. From there, Winfrey was hired as a co-anchor for the evening news at WJZ-TV, a station in Baltimore, but was dropped after only a few months and was instead given several other jobs such as writing and street reporting – where she constantly received negative feedback on her performance. Instead of quitting, Winfrey used the experience to recognize where her strengths lay and pivoted towards her values instead. She learned that although she loved working in television, she didn't like the news, and that while human interest stories were what she enjoyed the most, she just couldn't stay emotionally detached. Winfrey began co-hosting a small talk show with Richard Sher, something which most people at the time would consider a demotion from anchoring the news, but which set her on the path to host what would become *The Oprah Winfrey Show* in Chicago five years later. Winfrey followed her values to create a meaningful working life, which is a topic we'll dive deeper in to in Chapter 10.

Often when we think about the careers of successful people, it's hard to imagine how they started out, as we only see the success, not the failures along the way. No matter where you are in your career – just starting out, making a big change, working towards the next step, or slowing down – being mindful of your values and using them to guide you will give your working life meaning. When uncertainty strikes, challenges threaten your plans or unpredictable change completely shifts your working life, accepting your feelings and focusing on what matters to you – your values – can help to pull or push you towards your next career step.

Allowing thoughts to flow

Of course, in the process of pursuing a meaningful life, everyone will encounter barriers. Sometimes these are external to us and even at times outside of our control – such as health worries, potential redundancy on the horizon, and relationship issues, to name a few. There are, however, internal barriers that many of us experience, such as thoughts, feelings and memories that get in the way of what we want to achieve. In his book *The Happiness Trap*, Russ Harris teaches readers that the mind is made up of many cognitive processes, such as problem solving, remembering, visualizing, decision making and learning, all of which rely on the use of language – which is what we use to talk to ourselves in our heads.[4] This can be complicated, but it's an important part of the ACT theory, because understanding that your thoughts run through your head in a constant stream means you can notice them without being caught up in them. Put simply, your thoughts are not your mind. And your thoughts are not you as a person.

Imagine you experience a challenging event at work. Say you missed out on a promotion that went to a colleague. You may feel angry, disappointed, even sad about not being successful in your promotion, and in the circumstances those are completely understandable responses. This could affect your behaviour at work – with your colleague who got the role and with your manager who made the decision. You could also lose interest in your work. As we walked through previously in this chapter when delving into the cognitive behavioural coaching technique, you could change how you think about the situation. But there is also another option. You can view the thoughts as just that – a series of thoughts about the situation that are travelling through your mind. You don't have to change the thoughts, engage with them, ruminate on them, or direct them. Think of it as being a driver of a bus and your thoughts are rowdy passengers. They might be distracting, and even create an uncomfortable experience at times, but they will get off the bus at some point – your thoughts will pass.

Accepting the experience doesn't make it less painful. But it does alter the perspective – rather than using energy to change how you think and feel, you can acknowledge the uncomfortable feeling or pain, and hold on to the fact it will pass. This process can be described as looking at your thoughts – observing them and reflecting on what your thoughts are, rather than looking out on the world starting from the perspective of your thoughts. The aim isn't to remove thoughts or feel better. The aim is to reduce the influence of these thoughts on your behaviour.

relying on your values as your guiding light can be motivational and help you to move towards a meaningful life

While allowing your thoughts to flow, observing and not challenging them, if you focus on your values, and let what you want to stand for in life lead the way when you're deciding what steps to take next, you can find yourself in a position where you're navigating the uncomfortable and challenging feelings associated with uncertainty in a productive way. As Oprah Winfrey found out when she made her career move, which to the outside world seemed like a demotion, relying on your values as your guiding light can be motivational and help you to move towards a meaningful life – which is a way to stay focused on overcoming obstacles.

The agile emotional response plan

When we respond to challenges at work, we make choices, although it may not feel like it at the time. You can choose how you behave; you can consider what steps you take, and you can decide how you respond based on what you would like to get out of the situation. You can choose to adapt your emotional responses, as explored in CBT techniques, or you can decide to observe and accept your thoughts about a challenging situation, as directed by ACT theory process.

You may not master all approaches to dealing with emotions and thoughts immediately; it can take some time testing different strategies to determine what works for you. The key point to remember is, you have a choice. When faced with uncertainty, unpredictability and change, you will experience feelings and emotions about the event – that's part of being human and it's part of life. Managing your emotions at work isn't about minimizing or even eliminating emotions – that's not a healthy or effective approach. Rather, it's about building your self-awareness, understanding how you feel, and working with emotions in a way that is healthy, productive and effective for you. It can also be helpful to be flexible in how you manage your emotions. When reflecting on how your emotions have led to a behavioural response following a challenging event, ask yourself how you would like to navigate that process in the future. Will you focus on accepting the emotions you feel while at the same time committing to moving forward? Would you rather find a way to start viewing the situation differently, so you don't experience the same intense emotions? The choice is yours. And the choice should continue to be yours – there isn't one best way of managing your emotions at work.

Being flexible in your emotional response provides an opportunity to test what works for you, in specific situations. If you can view your approach to testing responses as an experiment – where you test a hypothesis and gather feedback – it can provide space to trial different ways to manage your emotions. Rather than chasing the end-goal of finding the right way for you to work with your emotions at work, an agile emotional response places the focus on choosing the best way to work with your emotions at one time, and that can change over time.

Practising mental agility

Part of developing cognitive flexibility is making choices in how you think about and respond to situations. This skill is also at the heart of what it takes to be mentally agile, which is the capacity to respond to events in a flexible way and be able to move quickly between different ideas. If you're mentally agile, you can navigate change and find the best course of action to move forward despite unpredictable events. It's not about having all the answers – but about being confident that you can figure out a new way of doing things to get where you want to go.

If you can learn to practise cognitive agility, whereby you're choosing how to process information and respond to events, you've mastered the first step of mental agility. In the unpredictable and uncertain workplace of today, mental agility will be one of the key skills required to create success and effectively overcome challenges, work through change and develop in your career. Gone are the days when we could start out on one fixed career path, accumulate the skills needed to execute that job effectively and progress up the career ladder. Today careers are shaped by how well we respond to changes in our company, industry and the global economy. We need to be adaptable not only to thrive in our careers, but at this point just to function effectively day-to-day. Mental agility has become a non-negotiable skill everyone needs at work, no matter what career path you're on, or your level of experience.

Mental agility has become a non-negotiable skill everyone needs at work

Developing mental agility can take some practice. It has four key stages (see Figure 4.1):

1 Cognitive flexibility sets the foundation of developing mental agility as you develop the ability to adapt and shift your thought process.
2 Nurturing a curious perspective is the next step in mental agility, and this is the process of remaining open to new ideas and embracing an inquisitive outlook to

FIGURE 4.1   The four stages in developing mental agility

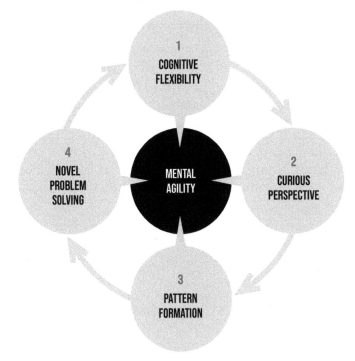

learn new information. In a continually changing working world, taking a curious approach to learning more about the world around you will inform the steps you take to navigate uncertainty.

3   The next stage of mental agility is pattern formation, which results from responding to multiple information points and connecting dots that may not be obvious, to map and model the information in an orderly format. Pattern formation is often a unique process, and you

may not create patterns in the same way as others, which is positive.

4 The final stage of mental agility is novel problem solving, which is the ability to create innovate outputs based on new procedures and processes to overcome challenges. Novel problem solving relates to the ability to examine problems in new ways and come up with new ways to tackle challenges.

At the heart of it, mental agility is the ability to view situations, absorb information, connect dots between ideas and use all the information you've assimilated to respond to changes around you in new and innovative ways, all of which are skills we need to thrive in an uncertain workplace.

Embracing failure

It's impossible to consider how emotions play a role at work without addressing failure – one of the biggest factors that can impact emotions. Nobody enjoys failing. Whether it's a small mistake in our day-to-day lives or something bigger that doesn't go our way, failure isn't something that anybody strives for. When we're small children, we learn that failure is part of the learning process – no one knows how to ride a bike immediately; we fall off, get back on and try again until we learn how to stay upright on two wheels. As we move into adulthood and pressure piles on, failing can start to feel like confirmation that we're not good enough and shouldn't keep working towards achieving something.

It's important to remember that we're not defined by our failures. Failure is inevitable, and even necessary. It can be a stepping-stone to success, and is often instrumental in helping us get where we want to be. The most successful people have usually overcome countless setbacks and disappointments before reaching career peaks – Walt Disney was fired from the *Kansas City Star* because his editor thought that he lacked imagination and good ideas, and Steve Jobs was very publicly fired from the company he founded, Apple.[5] Although this was described as a very painful experience in a biography by Walter Isaacson, he writes that Jobs didn't dwell on the discomfort for too long.[6] He swiftly co-founded NeXT, a computer company that Apple later bought, and he launched the worldwide brand that is Pixar Animation Studios. Remarkably, Jobs returned to Apple after a decade away from the business, at which point he led the brand-defining strategy into creating the iPod, iPhone and iPad. The failure of being fired wasn't the end of Jobs' story, it was part of it. How we view events that don't go to plan, or are challenging, is something we have control over, particularly if you're being flexible in how you manage your emotions.

Jack Ma, co-founder and former executive chairman of Alibaba Group, is one of the most influential business leaders in the world. He was named one of the 'world's 50 greatest leaders' by *Fortune* in 2017 and his company is a model for Chinese businesses and start-ups.[7] Before Alibaba took off, however, Ma faced a string of failures, something which Duncan Clark, in his book *Alibaba*, suggests prepared him for life as an entrepreneur.[8] He failed his college entrance exams three times before passing and was rejected by Harvard ten times. In his early twenties he applied for a job at KFC and was the only person who didn't get hired. In a public lecture at the University of Nairobi he said, 'If you cannot get used to failure – just like a boxer – if you can't get used to [being] hit, how can you win?... When you share a lot of failure stories, you learn.'[9]

Ma thinks it's important to learn to deal with failure and see it as an opportunity. When something doesn't work out, a different path opens itself up to you. If you can learn to view failure in this way and not allow it to say anything about your inherent worth, it will help you succeed. As Clark points out in his book, when speaking about his rejection from Harvard, Ma reflected on how amusing he finds the situation now and mused that maybe someday he should go and teach there. According to Ma, he now teaches his colleagues at Alibaba about failure and shares case studies about this, instead of reinforcing success.

Surviving failure helps build our resilience and makes us better equipped to tackle challenges and hardship in the future. It makes us more adept at dealing with change, solving problems and bouncing back from disappointments. Once we become comfortable with failure, we realize that most of the time it's not the end of the world, and that we can persevere with more insights than we had before or decide to go in a different direction. The lessons we take from our experiences with failure are what matter most.

When it comes to responding to failure, you can decide to embrace the discomfort and keep moving forward to learn from the process, or you can get stuck and wallow in the pain. We all work in an increasingly uncertain and unpredictable world, and that pattern is set to continue. The reality is we need to be able to react quickly to new situations, to pivot in the face of new obstacles, and to get comfortable with testing new ways of doing things when we don't have tried and tested methods to fall back on. In these circumstances, we won't always get it right; we may even fail. But rather than that process being something that causes self-doubt, dented confidence and shame, it can teach us how to do things even better in the future. That shift starts right at the point of managing your thoughts when you experience discomfort when plans haven't materialized as you'd hoped. You can choose to change your thinking to create a better outcome for you, or you can learn to accept your thoughts as images and words that you're experiencing to teach you something. Or you can choose to do both in different situations.

Failure makes us stronger

Throughout the process of creating her media empire, Oprah Winfrey has faced several public failures, all of which she credits for making her stronger. In 2011, following the Oprah Winfrey Network's debut, she faced harsh criticisms because of low ratings – but used this feedback to pivot again, taking on the role of CEO and turning the channel into a mainstay. In a Wellesley College commencement address Winfrey shared with students that she had been wounded many times in life, but had learned to turn wounds into wisdom, which is a brilliant example of building resilience using a growth mindset.[10]

In the next coaching chapter we'll explore exercises and strategies designed to develop cognitive flexibility, and to help you to deal with challenges and change at work effectively.

CHAPTER 05

Coaching:
The art of the everyday pivot

In today's working world, we have no choice but to adapt and respond to the changes surrounding us. Although the rate of change may have increased in some ways, the workplace has always been evolving. The difference today is the speed with which we need to respond in order to remain productive and effective in our roles. This is where the everyday pivot plays an important role in our working lives – if you can learn to respond to your environment and make small changes frequently, you're more likely to perform at your peak, navigate obstacles quickly and effectively, and ultimately thrive in your working life.

Navigating change and unpredictability isn't a comfortable process for everyone; we all have different tolerance levels for uncertainty. One way to broaden your tolerance for change is to make small, simple improvement tweaks part of your everyday life, focusing on a slight change of direction – a pivot – in areas where this makes sense to achieve slightly better outcomes.

The idea of a pivot isn't just a fancy way of rebranding the process of making changes in your life. A pivot has two meanings: a point on which something rests and turns; and something that is central or important to someone or something else. A pivot can feel psychologically easier than making a big change, as it can be a small twist or turn in a slightly different direction. Let me provide you with an example where I've had to make a pivot in two directions recently. I've been writing a bi-weekly newsletter, *Mindset Matters*, on LinkedIn for over 18 months; the engagement and subscriber levels are high.[1] The newsletters are designed to provide practical tips for those that want to thrive in their careers, so I started to consider whether I should increase the newsletter to every week, as it's clearly making an impact. My thinking was that I should perhaps provide more coaching tips to help people navigate the new world of work. So, I pivoted – I trialled publishing the newsletter every week.

This wasn't a huge change. I didn't need a new strategy or process, I just needed to do more of what I was doing. It was, however, a change to my workload. I hadn't realized until I started publishing it every week how much energy the newsletter requires, and I benefit from having a week in between newsletters to focus on other ways to communicate, such as running live coaching events. I found that I wasn't getting time to rest in between newsletters, and over the long term that could impact my interaction with those that engage with the newsletter. I didn't want to have to pull back from replying to those who had questions, needed more support or wanted to comment. And I found engagement and subscriber levels did not increase when I published every week versus every other week. So, I pivoted back to my original strategy of writing a good-quality newsletter every other week and providing substantial levels of support around that topic for two weeks, until the next newsletter is published.

It's important to experiment with new strategies and ideas, but you need to understand and interpret the data about the change when you're doing this. What are the analytics showing you? What feedback have you received from others? Are you listening to feedback from yourself? In this case, my wellbeing and energy levels suffered, which meant I couldn't continue the level of support I had previously been providing.

When I was thinking about how I should map out my newsletter publishing strategy, if I'd jumped straight into thinking about the *big* changes I could or should make, I would have avoided the process, and most likely not tested any new ideas. On the face of it, this may seem like a positive – after all, didn't I just revert to my original strategy anyway? However, not testing a new approach would have been a terrible idea. I wouldn't have learned anything about the process – either about myself and my ability to help others, or the metrics I could compare from a weekly versus bi-weekly newsletter.

I debated whether to use this example. It feels like a mundane way to illustrate an everyday pivot. But that is *completely* the point – the everyday pivot is hardly ever exciting, grand or ground-breaking. But the results can be over time. Take the decision I made to start a newsletter – the Covid-19 pandemic was just starting to take hold, and we were just about to go into our first lockdown in the UK – something most people had never experienced before. When new LinkedIn newsletter functionality was launched, it seemed like the perfect opportunity to share what I know about navigating uncertainty to help people get through a tricky time in the workplace. I was already sharing similar information in other ways, so this was a pivot, a small change in direction, an experiment to some extent. I set out to test the process and determine whether I could help people, and the effort paid off as the newsletter became one of the fastest-growing subscriber newsletters on LinkedIn. That doesn't mean I find publishing a newsletter easy – far from it. I find writing very difficult at times. Creating a newsletter takes a huge amount of time and effort, and I'm distilling almost two decades' worth of expertise into what I'm writing. But the decision to experiment with the process was easy.

Of course, your working life will probably look very different to mine, but there will most certainly be ways you can master the everyday pivot to boost your performance, productivity and wellbeing. Once you master the art of the pivot, apply it to your working life to create results.

◎ REFRAMING THOUGHTS EXERCISE

At the heart of it, cognitive flexibility is the ability to adjust thinking patterns to adapt to new conditions or create a better outcome – either for yourself or others. Those that are cognitively flexible can adjust their thinking and shift their understanding of situations. They've mastered the art of reframing thoughts.

As you may remember, in Chapter 4 I explored the ABCDE cognitive reframing model. Now is your chance to practise this technique for yourself and take some time to consider how you might reframe your thinking about a current challenge you're facing. This model utilizes the evidence-based techniques of cognitive behavioural therapy (CBT).

Use the template in Table 5.1 to map out the situation. I'll walk you through an example – imagine you're completing the template based on this example.

Step 1 – first, note the activating event in a factual way. Be mindful not to include why the event happened, how you felt, or observations about other people – just stick to the objective facts. Write this as if you were a reporter detailing the event, so:

- In the team meeting David stated that my team haven't delivered on our targets again.

Next detail your beliefs, which could include:

- We're always the scapegoat for David's team.
- David insists on shifting the blame to portray himself in a better light and devalue my work.
- This approach isn't fair, collaborative or accurate.

Next up state the consequences:

- I lost my temper with David in the meeting and looked unprofessional in front of the wider team.

TABLE 5.1   ABCDE exercise template

Step 1		
Activating event	**B**eliefs	**C**onsequences
◦	◦	◦
	◦	◦
	◦	◦

Step 2	
Disrupting thought	**E**ffective new approach
◦	◦
	◦
	◦

- My self-confidence is dwindling as this isn't the first time I've faced this criticism in a team meeting.
- My relationship with David is starting to feel irreparable and I now have tension with my manager who didn't appreciate my outburst.

Through this process you're detailing the stages of how the event unfolded, and it's clear how your beliefs about the situation led to the consequences. David's actions may not have helped, but his criticism did not cause the outburst in the meeting – that was based on how you felt about the situation and your beliefs about David's behaviour.

Step 2 – challenge your perception of the events to reach a better outcome. If you replayed the situation, how could you change your beliefs to lessen the negative outcome? For example, you could change your beliefs to:

- Maybe David is lashing out and showing his vulnerability. This isn't a reflection on my team or my competence as a leader.
- I don't know what David's intention is, but I can take control of my reaction.
- This isn't the way I would approach this situation and I don't have to use the same tactics; I want to be seen as reasonable and calm.

Then imagine if this played out, and how the situation would unfold without you losing your temper and allowing the situation to knock your confidence:

- I calmly state that isn't how the situation unfolded from my perspective, and I can add more context to the story to provide further insight.

- I detail the facts, illustrating where David is factually incorrect and tell the team I know we can learn from the situation, and my team would be open to making changes.
- I offer to meet with David later to discuss events in more detail. This way, the group know David's version of events isn't necessarily the whole story, but I'm not going to hijack the meeting to discuss it.

You can look back at past events to identify how you could shift your thinking, and also work through this exercise in real time to determine how you can respond to current challenges in new and effective ways. This approach does require you to take a breath before automatically responding to events, and techniques such as stepping away from the situation, waiting for cortisol levels to drop in your body (so feelings such as anger subside), or practising a breathing exercise can help with this.

◉ OBSERVE YOUR THOUGHTS EXERCISE

Although reframing your thinking (CBT) is an evidence-based and effective approach to navigating challenges, sometimes you may achieve a better outcome by learning to observe your thoughts (acceptance and commitment therapy, ACT). This is another evidence-based approach.

Whereas reframing thoughts focuses on *changing* thinking patterns, the opposite approach whereby you notice and observe your thoughts and *don't change* the way you think and process information can also be an effective way to navigate uncertainty. Both approaches are grounded in extensive research and proven results; the key is to understand them both and, in the spirit of cognitive flexibility, be adaptable and decide which is the best one to use in different situations you find yourself in.

If you can learn to view your thoughts as ideas that are passing through your mind, and understand that your thoughts are not who you are, it can make it easier to deal with some of the thinking you do that is challenging. So, if we take the last example of your colleague David being critical of your team in a meeting, rather than working to reframe your thinking to change how you react, you could look at your thoughts as something you're experiencing that you don't need to react to. You may say to yourself:

- I'm experiencing the thought that we're always the scapegoat for David's team.
- I'm experiencing the thought that David insists on shifting the blame to portray himself in a better light and devalue my work.
- I'm experiencing the thought that this approach isn't fair, collaborative or accurate.

The switch here to acknowledging your thoughts *as thoughts* – not facts and not a reflection of you as a person – distances you slightly from the thinking and can make the experience less intense. You can learn to accept your thoughts, acknowledge they're not a threat, and continue to move towards meaningful goals for you – thoughts do not have to disrupt that journey. At times, thoughts will be unpleasant, painful or challenging, and you don't always need to change that process. Thoughts come and go and change over time. Sometimes acknowledging your thoughts, being clear they don't define you and finding ways to keep progressing can be a useful way to navigate difficult situations.

Understanding when to work at adapting your thinking and when to accept and observe your thinking patterns is part of the process of developing cognitive flexibility. This may take some testing, and learning what works for you and what doesn't. You may also want to consider where you invest your energy. Changing your thinking style requires persistence, motivation and ultimately a significant amount of energy, so you may find you use this process when the stakes are high or it's important that you change an outcome. The rest of the time you might want to work on accepting and observing your thoughts helping you to move forward despite navigating uncertainty and discomfort.

◉ BUSTING CONFIRMATION BIAS EXERCISE

We can process huge amounts of information quickly and efficiently because we use cognitive shortcuts that help to sort, process and store information. This is an incredibly useful process; without it we would be overwhelmed with the amount of information bombarding our senses every second. The downside, however, is these shortcuts create biases – we process information (mostly subconsciously) in tried and tested ways, and we don't often adapt or alter that process.

Confirmation bias is the process whereby we interpret information as confirmation of existing beliefs. So, think back to the example of the difficult interaction with David. Your beliefs about the situation could be confirming what you expect to happen – maybe you expect David to devalue the work your team produce because of his competitive nature. If you're *expecting* this, that's how you'll interpret the situation. What if this isn't what your colleague was intending? What if David's observation was correct this time and your team had dropped the ball? By lashing out in a meeting you may be demonstrating to other team members that you're not willing to take feedback on board and work on a solution to find a better outcome.

When it comes to problem solving, challenge yourself to seek out alternative arguments and ideas. Don't fall into the trap of responding in the same way you always have. Pause before deciding how to tackle a challenge, and ask yourself these questions:

- How could someone else tackle this? (You can think of a specific person.)
- What are all the possible ways I could overcome this challenge?
- What is the opposite approach to the one I would like to take?

You don't have to use any of the ideas you come up with; indeed, you may decide to stick with your original plan. The point is, you're challenging yourself to consider alternative perspectives, ideas and approaches, and at some point you may choose one of these. You're demonstrating the ability to shift your thinking and take in information that contradicts your viewpoint. You're shining a light on your cognitive blind spots. And if you don't go with one of these alternative approaches to solving problems, you're strengthening the argument as to why you're taking the approach you've chosen.

◉ NURTURE A CURIOUS MINDSET EXERCISE

If you want to understand alternative ways of viewing the world, you must actively seek out perspectives that challenge your own. This isn't always an easy process. Often we're comfortable with our own view of the world, and challenging our beliefs can feel threatening at times. We've evolved as humans to be comfortable with what we know, because it feels safe. This is, however, an illusion. Just because you haven't acknowledged other ways of interpreting events, it doesn't mean those points of view don't exist.

The desire to feel safe and to be able to control our future is part of what makes navigating change and uncertainty so unpleasant and challenging at times. However, not knowing how events will unfold and not always being able to direct situations are part of our reality in work, and in life. Nurturing a way of thinking – a mindset – that empowers you to navigate uncertainty, even when it isn't desirable, will provide you with skills you need to deal with change in the future. One of the most effective ways to do this is to nurture curiosity, taking yourself outside of your thinking 'comfort zone', challenging your beliefs and reminding yourself there are many effective and alternative ways to respond to events, and there are many ways that people can view and process information. In short, this process turns uncertainty into a positive situation whereby you can learn from others or from events.

Here are some ways you can incorporate curiosity into your life:

- Read news articles from various sources – not just your preferred source.

- Try new activities you've never experienced before, not with the intention of becoming an expert at something new, just to learn and try a new experience.
- Before tackling a challenge, ask other people how they would respond – even those who you know would respond differently to you (in fact, especially these people).
- Consider people you admire – how could you learn from them? Maybe you could read their work, join a club they're part of, connect with them, follow their work somehow.
- Relentlessly ask questions. Rather than falling into the trap of doing things the easy way as they've always been done, ask yourself and others why this is the case. Emulate a curious five-year-old, viewing the world without preconceived ideas and asking questions.
- Read, watch, or listen to different types of material. If you're into reading non-fiction, try a novel. If you enjoy podcasts, challenge yourself to try different kinds of podcast.
- Seek out people of interest. This could be via social media or using an online search engine. For example, if you're interested in engineering, find people to follow in that field.
- Visit a physical bookstore or library and browse the shelves.
- Focus on mysteries that may not have a definitive answer, rather than puzzles that have a fixed way of achieving results. The point is to embrace ambiguity.
- Even as an expert, be interested in everything. You may have extensive knowledge, but there is always more to learn about your area of expertise, or other areas

that may spark ideas about how you can tackle a new challenge.

· Commit to learning a new skill – this could be a professional skill, something that just interests you as a hobby, or working on mindset skills (covered in this book).

A curious mindset can help you to creatively approach challenges, become more comfortable with ambiguity and uncertainty, and focus on developing new ways of doing things.

◉ EMBRACE NOVELTY EXERCISE

Novelty breeds adaptability. If you consider what it takes to be adaptable, you need to appreciate and nurture alternative perspectives and be open to testing new approaches. Novelty embraces curiosity, and at the heart of it is embracing new or original experiences or ideas. By strategically building novelty into your life you can boost cognitive flexibility.

Over time, you will face change at work, perhaps even extreme change. You will also be exposed to challenges, again, perhaps extreme. Planning or hoping for a stable working environment is fruitless in today's complex and uncertain working world. A more effective approach to career planning is to prepare yourself to deal with change and minimize the discomfort that can be experienced with uncertainty.

One of the simplest and most effective ways of bringing novelty into your life is to build on a curious mindset and purposely change some of your regular routines and processes. Although there's a lot to be said for incorporating tried and tested practices into your life to minimize the amount of time and energy it takes to make decisions, purposely changing these practices over time can focus your awareness on new ways of doing things.

Take the well-documented strategy of wearing the same style of clothing every day to make the process of getting dressed quickly, without having to draw on any energy you need for bigger decisions later in the day – Steve Jobs was reported to be a fan of this approach, and Mark Zuckerberg generally wears the same work uniform every day. This is a sensible approach to reduce decision fatigue, but if you want to introduce some novelty into your life, you might want to explore changing this routine from time to time. The same could apply to commuting routes, for those that go into an office or workplace. We often take the same route, but what if you took a different turn? Or walked down a different road? Got off at a different train or bus stop? You may notice something different or learn something new that could spark creativity.

These examples seem inconsequential and perhaps pointless. But these small changes that don't necessarily have an end-goal can help you to look at the world differently and come up with new ideas. Embracing novelty in a small way can start a habit that can result in practising novelty in a big way. As your thinking becomes more flexible, you can bend, shape and stretch your thought process, and this can help to boost creativity and innovation in the workplace, where you can generate novel and original ideas, and find ways to make those ideas a reality.

Here are some ideas for how you can start to embrace 'micro-novelty' moments:

- Change your usual route to work or places you attend regularly.
- Try different styles of cooking with ingredients you don't normally use.
- Work from different places (if this is an option for you).
- Revise some of your working processes, and consider if you were starting the process again how you would change it.
- Switch up your lunchtime routine – do something different.
- Connect with colleagues you don't usually check-in with.

Coupling a novel approach (changing routines) with a curious mindset (taking in new information, which we explored in the last exercise) will help you to feel empowered to problem solve and find new solutions when you face obstacles and uncertainty.

◎ STRATEGIZING NEW SOLUTIONS EXERCISE

As discussed in Chapter 4, there are four factors that together build mental agility. Learning to harness these factors together will help you to formulate solutions when you come up against challenges or need to navigate new situations.

The first factor is cognitive flexibility, which we've explored in this coaching chapter, and this focuses on being flexible in how you think and process information.

The second factor is a curious perspective, which encompasses challenging yourself to view the world in a different way to the norm for you and incorporating novelty into your day-to-day life.

The third factor is pattern formation, and this is the process of categorizing and sorting information based on what you've learned from practising cognitive flexibility and nurturing a curious perspective. You could find, for example, that reading news from sources you don't usually subscribe to has brought to your attention an interesting development in an industry you don't work within. Although this doesn't relate to your work, there could be elements of the development that relate to you – such as building a community within a client base, utilizing artificial intelligence tools to enhance efficiency, or using a productivity tool to support team projects. The possibilities here are endless. Pattern formation will occur as you consider new information you're learning and start to connect the possibilities between this new information and your current world. You may also find yourself in the position of connecting the dots between new concepts and ideas you're learning about, which combined could impact the way you work.

The fourth and final part of building mental agility is novel problem solving – coming up with new and original ways of doing things. This part requires you to have built competency in the other three areas of mental agility, but it also helps you to start the cycle again – once you become proficient at novel problem solving, this will strengthen your cognitive flexibility and ability to challenge your thinking patterns and processes.

The next time that you have a problem to solve, or a choice to make about the steps you take, don't rush to create a solution, unless it's urgent or critical that you do so. Strategizing new solutions takes time and conscious effort, but the results will be more effective, influential and innovative than following a tried and tested action based on outdated assumptions and processes.

The first step is to consciously work through possible solutions. Ask yourself questions such as:

What are my initial thoughts about tackling this situation?

↓

How would other people tackle this issue?

↓

What are all the possible ways I could create a solution?

↓

What are the opposite approaches to those I would usually take?

↓

Based on comparing my approach to other potential approaches, what are my assumptions about this situation?

↓

Based on comparing my approach to other potential approaches, what are my biases?

↓

Who could I speak with to get an alternative perspective on the situation and potential solutions?

Take some time to challenge yourself with these questions – this shouldn't be an easy exercise. Sit with the answers for a while before deciding what to do next.

The second step is to create space. There's a reason your best ideas come to you when you're in the shower, or jogging. I've recently experienced the situation where two solutions have occurred to me, one in the shower, and one in the gym. I wasn't consciously trying to figure out either situation, but I had been working on problem solving in the days before these events happened, and it was in the quiet time where I was consciously focused on something else that my brain subconsciously made a connection between ideas.

You need to allow yourself space to process information consciously (where you know you're working on figuring out the problem) and subconsciously (where your brain is processing information in the background without you being aware) before deciding on your strategy. As far as I'm aware, there's no published data in the field of neuro-psychology that states the optimum amount of time to allow for subconscious processing, so it can be tricky to account for this time – do you give yourself a day? A week? A month? There isn't a definitive answer to this; it's important to allow your brain some time to rest from considering the problem you're trying to solve, so factor this in how you can.

I recommend working on the problem for a while and mixing that time with alternative mental activities that help you to work in your flow and switch off from the issue you're working on. (Exercises in Chapter 3 can help you to find your flow.) You won't always have ideas come to you subconsciously, but by allowing yourself some space and time for this to happen, you're being strategic about finding new solutions.

It's important to give yourself a deadline – you won't always have the luxury of taking huge amounts of time to decide. When you hit that time deadline, create a plan based on the information you have. This can change later

– as conditions change, your strategy needs to change. A static strategy isn't a useful career development tool – you need to be able to adapt your strategy regularly based on changing information and circumstances.

When you're ready to choose your direction, you need a plan of action, which includes your vision about what you want to achieve, detailed goals outlining milestones, and exact tactics you'll deploy to reach your goals. You can use the template in Table 5.2 to help with this. Start by outlining your vision – where you want to be. Then write down tangible goals that will help you to reach that vision, and for each goal add action steps, which are your tactics – the things you'll do to reach this goal.

The exercises in this chapter will help you to build your cognitive flexibility – a key skill required to navigate changeable, uncertain and complex workplaces. In the next chapter we'll be delving into another key skill you need to thrive at work today – a growth mindset. This outlook is such a hot topic at work that many organizations are incorporating the concept of a growth mindset into their core values, placing this way of thinking at the heart of career success. Join me in Chapter 6 where I'll explain why this concept is so critical today at work, no matter where you are on your career journey, and how you can start to nurture your growth mindset.

TABLE 5.2   Vision, goals and tactics template

Vision	

Goal	Tactics
⬡	⬡
	⬡
	⬡
Goal	**Tactics**
⬡	⬡
	⬡
	⬡
Goal	**Tactics**
⬡	⬡
	⬡
	⬡
Goal	**Tactics**
⬡	⬡
	⬡
	⬡
Goal	**Tactics**
⬡	⬡
	⬡
	⬡

CHAPTER 06

A growth mindset

Picture the scene. You've just been interviewed for a job you really want. You walk out of the interview feeling pleased with how it went, and you're hopeful you'll be offered the role. The following week, you receive a call from the recruiter to say although the interview went well, you didn't get the job – it went to someone else with more experience. Deep down, you know you had the experience to do the role, and you know you would have been a great fit. But nerves got the better of you, and in hindsight you reflect that you didn't showcase your talents and experience to the best of your ability.

If you have a fixed mindset, you might think to yourself you'll *never* be offered a role like this, you just can't manage your nerves and keep them in check in interviews. It feels like an exam to you, and you just can't get over that. This could reflect a fixed mindset, a term documented by Carol Dweck in her book *Mindset*, which suggests those with a fixed mindset believe their skills and abilities won't change over time.[1] Those with a fixed mindset believe they achieve a level of ability that is capped and can't be extended any further. In the interview scenario, if you had a fixed mindset about the situation, you would feel that there's nothing more you can do in interviews, and you can never get any better at the process.

As pointed out by Dweck, a growth mindset is a completely opposite perspective to a fixed mindset. If you had received the bad news about not getting a role, and you adopted a growth mindset, you might see the experience as an opportunity to learn and get better at the process. After all, you *know* you have the experience, so it's just a matter of finding a way to express that. With a growth mindset, you may look at the situation like most of the work is done, it's not like you need to get experience – you've done that work. It's just the expression part you need to work on, and you can do that – you just need to learn how. It doesn't mean you're not disappointed with the outcome, it means you will use the experience to try to create a different outcome in the future.

And here's the thing, you can learn to interview well. You can practise providing examples, you can develop techniques to help you manage your nerves. This is because those with a growth mindset believe talent and ability aren't set in stone. In fact, not only can ability and competence levels change over time, but we can also actively plan to make this happen and achieve better results in the areas that matter to us.

Put simply, a growth mindset is all about lifelong learning and believing in your ability to develop skills and grow abilities over time. If you consider how uncertainty and change have become a permanent fixture in our working lives, it's clear why individuals that focus on continuous improvement and learning are likely to navigate uncertainty more successfully than those without this focus. If you want to succeed and perform well in today's workplace, you have no choice but to embrace learning – the world is changing so quickly that we must learn as we go. While some enjoy this process, for others it can be a challenge to let go of some of the stability we once expected from a career.

embrace learning – the world is changing so quickly that we must learn as we go.

Fixed, growth and mixed mindsets

Traditionally, research focused on exploring fixed and growth mindsets, and not so much in between.[2] But what if you find you have a growth mindset in some areas – such as finding ways to build new sales leads at work – but are fixed in your mindset in other ways – such as believing you wouldn't be able to enhance your emotional intelligence, even if it meant you could foster stronger relationships at work? Where does this leave you when it comes to classifying your mindset? Well, maybe you have a mixed mindset, which means sometimes you're fixed in your views on not being able to develop and change, and other times you believe you can grow and develop your skills and abilities in a particular situation or context. This illustrates why it's so important to consider how research applies to real life – it's about translating research into a pragmatic approach that works in the real world – and, more importantly, *your world*. Many of us have a mixed mindset at work, which means how we think about a situation will be shaped by the environment and context around us.

It doesn't matter whether you currently have a fixed or mixed mindset, everyone can develop a growth mindset. Even if you consider yourself to have a growth mindset right now, the nature of that style of thinking is always learning more, so the focus should be using strategies to keep nurturing a growth mindset. The concept of working with a growth mindset is so critical in the workplace today, that Satya Nadella, the CEO of Microsoft, has woven a growth mindset into the Microsoft culture.[3]

Microsoft credits its record growth in the last several years to applying a growth mindset, so much so that they introduced a programme called Model Coach Care to instil the concept of a growth mindset in managers across the company at scale. When Nadella became CEO in 2014, the company was struggling and stagnant, in part due to its rigid and inflexible culture. Nadella knew that to turn company performance around, culture change was needed first. He pushed the business from being a place where employees felt like they needed to be the sole source of knowledge, where proving oneself was crucial, and where hierarchy made it difficult to tap into existing creativity across the business, into a company that thrives on collaboration and breeds innovation and talent – all thanks to a growth mindset. According to Nadella, a 'learn-it-all' employee is more successful and valuable than a 'know-it-all', which is why he encouraged Microsoft employees to think of themselves as students rather than experts, in order to change the company culture.

As Nadella knows, fostering a growth mindset can dramatically improve performance, as teams become hubs for learning and creativity. It also reduces the pressure to always find the right solutions to challenges immediately. Rather, a growth mindset promotes smart experimentation, boosting innovation in the process. A growth mindset also debunks the idea that there is one correct solution for each challenge; there are often many ways to address a new situation, and the solution that works right now may be different in the future as the context changes.

Research has also supported the benefits of fostering a growth mindset over a fixed mindset. Schroder and colleagues studied anxiety and found those with fixed anxiety mindsets felt that situations that caused anxiety were out of their control.[4] On the flip side, those with growth anxiety mindsets were more likely to view anxious situations as changeable in a positive way. Those with a growth mindset were more likely to cope with stressful life events, and less likely to experience negative health effects such as depression because of trauma or stress. Not only can a growth mindset help individuals to keep moving forward creatively while dealing with new business demands; it can also promote better psychological health.

So, imagine you're in the process of navigating a merger at work, and your role is changing, but how significant that change will be is unclear. Not knowing what the future holds can be stressful and extremely challenging – as humans we've evolved to enjoy being in a position where we can predict what comes next. Those with a fixed mindset may focus on what they're losing – stability, predictability and safety – and their thoughts may quickly go towards what will happen when they lose their jobs, even though that hasn't been communicated as an option. I've coached people who hate their jobs prior to a merger, but dislike the unpredictability experienced in a merger even more than the job they dislike. It turns out that dislike of unpredictability can trump dislike of a job at times.

Your mindset has the power to change your game at work, and in your personal life.

If you have a growth mindset and experience this situation, it doesn't make the event more desirable – you may not *choose* to be in this situation. Rather, it means you can accept that it's a challenging time and stay open to future opportunities that may come your way – there may be an opportunity to grow in your career, develop new skills, or learn from new leaders you've never been exposed to before. This isn't about ignoring the potential negative impact this event may have on your life, it's about taking a balanced view and choosing optimism where you can – promoting better mental health.

At the heart of adopting a growth mindset is the understanding that you can develop skills, abilities and talents over time. You have control of directing your mindset with effort and focus. Your mindset has the power to change your game at work, and in your personal life.

The talent trap

Taking pride in natural talents shouldn't be encouraged, according to Jeff Bezos, the founder of Amazon.[5] At first glance, this may seem like a strange comment to make, but Bezos explains that natural gifts should be celebrated, but we also need to acknowledge there's some luck involved – we're born with these gifts. Pride should be applauded when it's associated with choices someone has made to use their gifts – such as studying hard, working hard and practising repeatedly.

You've more than likely come across someone who has huge amounts of talent – whether that be athletic, academic, musical, artistic – and yet they've never achieved their potential because they haven't sharpened their skills, honed their talent, or worked to achieve more. And, on the flip side, there are people with a moderate amount of talent who work relentlessly to turn that into an achievement – they learn how to get better and take action to hone their skills. According to Bezos, you don't get to decide what your talents are, but you get to decide how hard you work at enhancing that talent. The choice is in your control, and the people that really excel are those that combine gifts and hard work.

Relying on talent alone to reach your goals is a trap, and if doing this is your plan to help you develop your career, you may be falling into a fixed mindset. Imagine you're an aspiring leader and you want to push yourself to achieve more. If you believe there's a limit to your skills and abilities, how are you going to push yourself beyond this level of competence, which is something all great leaders do consistently? In his book *Bounce*, the Olympian Matthew Syed explored how one small street in a suburban town in England produced more top table tennis players than the rest of the country combined when he was growing up.[6] How could it be that this one street just happened to be home to kids who were exceptionally talented? The answer is – it wasn't. Rather, a significant proportion of children in this area joined a table tennis group, where practising the sport became a part of their lives. Syed found this example

Relying on existing skills and abilities to achieve results won't motivate you to learn more

repeated time and time again as he researched how psychology and neuroscience promote goal achievement – a certain amount of natural talent can help, but the ingredient for success is practice *plus* talent. Ultimately, talent is overrated: there are more important factors that create success.

Consider something you want to achieve – maybe it's a career change, a qualification, or a promotion. If you categorize your abilities and skills as either present or not, and out of your control, this can edge you towards a fixed mindset and limit your potential to stretch your ability to reach goals and achieve more. In effect, you are limiting yourself, you're putting the brakes on your progress. Relying on existing skills and abilities to achieve results won't motivate you to learn more, develop your talents and skills, or reach your potential.

Developing new skills for work

Those who are performing well and have a fixed mindset can become complacent, assuming the talent they have will keep them at the top of their game. But this is risky in today's workplace. The skills we need to perform in our careers are changing, because the landscape at work is changing. A focus on workplace skills such as digital fluency, data analysis and AI has emerged as technological advancements shape our lives. There are personal skills or life skills that we will also need to nurture and hone if we're to navigate an uncertain and changeable working environment in a productive and healthy way – and this is where your mindset comes into play. According to the World Economic Forum, enhancing resilience, developing emotional intelligence and practising adaptability are all skills we need to today, because the workplace has changed so dramatically over the past few decades.[7] We need resilience to deal with challenges and resist being knocked off course, we need emotional intelligence to build strong relationships in increasingly complex working environments, and we need to be masters in agility to be able to pivot and change course when the world around us changes. You may have a talent in one of these areas, which will potentially play to your advantage, but it also may not. What happens when the next skills of the future workplace emerge, and you don't have natural talents in those areas, and you're used to relying on innate talent to propel you forward in your career?

This explains why relying on talent alone is a trap. You may see some progress, but you're missing the key ingredients that help you to push your potential even further – practice, persistence and focus. Nurturing a growth mindset doesn't eliminate the talent factor; there's no doubt that talent is an excellent launch pad for achievement. If you're lucky enough to have a talent that's a passion, focusing on developing skills associated with that talent can often help to create a sense of fulfilment. As we enter an increasingly uncertain world, however, the foundation of your growth mindset will be based on matching that talent with learning, and practice will be the critical step. This focus will help you to thrive in a complicated and uncertain working world.

An average level of talent, ability or skill isn't a hindrance when it comes to developing yourself – in fact this can be an advantage. Having some skill but knowing you can work hard to hone that skill can result in learning and development becoming a habit. On the flip side, sometimes those that have high levels of skill become used to relying on that innate talent to perform, which can often be enough to perform well. However, when it isn't enough, learning how to push your comfort zone to develop a little further can be an uncomfortable experience when this isn't a practice you're used to.

Creating a growth mindset helps you to understand that, no matter what challenges, changes or complexity are thrown your way, you can focus on learning and testing new ways of doing things to keep moving forward.

Lifelong learning

Success is a journey that starts and ends with continuous development. Former First Lady of the United States Michelle Obama has discussed her views on the power of learning and harnessing a growth mindset in her book *Becoming*.[8] Obama explains she realized early on that it was hard work not natural talent that leads to success. She mentions that often she wasn't the smartest person in the class and had to put in a lot more effort compared with others to achieve what she wanted to. She had to learn in order to be successful.

The first time Obama took the bar exam, she failed. Rather than feeling like she wasn't good enough, Obama chose to think she just wasn't good enough *yet*, but she could learn to be with more studying. With this attitude fuelling her focus, Obama passed the bar exam at her second attempt. This is a lesson Obama shares often – if you work hard, and put in the effort to learn more, you can realize huge achievements.

If you want to succeed and progress in a working world that continues to evolve, it's essential to focus on lifelong learning. Whereas in the past it may have been commonplace to focus on learning until you achieved a role you were happy to stay in for the long haul, in today's workplace that approach just won't cut it. Leaders can no longer rely on experience alone to forge new paths forward – the leadership skills they've honed may become ineffective or obsolete as the workplace changes.

Take hybrid and virtual working leadership, for example. Leaders will need new strategies, tools and skills to effectively manage teams that work in different ways if they haven't encountered this scenario before. Even if you're not leading teams, the career or role you're working towards will likely not remain static – to create success, you will need to be consistently acquiring new knowledge to stay on top of industry developments. You'll also need to be curious and open to exploring how your working environment is changing, focusing on understanding why these developments are occurring. It's hard to thrive in an environment that you don't understand. No matter where you are in an organization, or how far into your career you are, a learning mindset needs to be a staple in your toolkit that helps you to navigate change and uncertainty.

The failure advantage

Jeff Bezos is ranked first on *Forbes*' list of the wealthiest people in the world and has turned Amazon from an online bookseller in 1994 to an e-commerce giant today.[9] However, in his early years of business, Bezos had almost a billion dollars in failures.[10] Instead of letting these deter him and his vision, he took lessons from them to change course. Many of his words and actions make it clear that this is due to the value he places on continual learning and using mistakes to gain knowledge, adapt and grow.

Part of any kind of growth entails barriers being pushed and an entry into uncharted territory. When you're in the process of utilizing a growth mindset, you're entering a place that's unknown to you. As you take on novel challenges, attempt to find new solutions, or focus on broadening your understanding, you won't always be successful in achieving what you set out to do right away, in fact you may feel like you've failed, which can be uncomfortable to experience.

You may have come across stories about Thomas Edison, the inventor of the electric light bulb and motion pictures. His sophisticated research practices have informed those undertaken by research and development labs across the world today. According to the Edison Foundation, Edison was an early example of someone with a growth mindset and focus on lifelong learning. He worked following key principles that had been taught to him by his mother. These included never being discouraged by failure, but using that as a learning experience and springboard from which to keep trying the next approach. He also advocated learning theoretically from books, but also learning in a practical way, by testing new approaches.

Edison was never deterred by failure; in fact, he didn't view failure in the way many of us do today. For Edison, it was all part of the experimentation process, and understanding what doesn't work (and why) moves you one step closer to discovering a solution that does work. When Edison made the decision that a result was worth achieving, he continued with his experimental approach, testing new hypotheses and ideas until he learned what was going to work. He was what Satya Nadella, the CEO of Microsoft, would today call a learn-it-all, which is far superior in value to an organization than a know-it-all.[11] When it comes to thriving in uncertainty, an experimental mindset will be your superpower.

Mistakes, failure and challenges can be used to your advantage if you can shift your perspective to view these events as part of the process of reaching an effective and positive solution. This can feel easier if you focus on the rewards you'll achieve when you find a viable solution – which could include broadening your knowledge, developing skills, advancing your professional or personal development. At times, expanding your knowledge and overcoming challenges will be smooth sailing, whereas at other times there may be bumps in the road. The key is to prepare yourself for potential challenges and accept that you may at times fail as you start to explore new ideas, practise newly acquired skills and understand it's a normal part of the development process if all your decisions don't pay off.

When it comes to thriving in uncertainty, an experimental mindset will be your superpower.

In fact, it can be a positive approach to start celebrating failure, which is a common practice at pharmaceutical giant Lilly. Renowned for the focus on innovation where medicines are developed and approved at speed compared to competitors, the culture at Lilly has one component that isn't replicated by other pharmaceutical companies. The senior leadership teams embrace failure as an inevitable part of the innovation process and scientists are actively encouraged to take risks.[12] When scientists find a drug they're developing doesn't work out, rather than give up, they're encouraged to find other uses for it. In the 1990s, Lilly's chief scientific officer, W Leigh Thompson, initiated failure parties whereby the scientific process rather than the outcome was celebrated and applauded.

In the workplace today and in the future, learning to fail is critical. Although the Facebook culture of 'move fast and break things' – whereby the speed at which new products can be created is negatively weighted against governance – may be outdated,[13] in part because shareholders and customers are taking an interest in social impact, we still need to learn how to navigate the murky and sometimes ugly territory of publicly learning about what works as our environments change. That may require individuals to find a way to fail, make mistakes and struggle with complexities of new challenges without feeling over-whelmed or embarrassed, which can be supported by focusing on the process, rather than the outcome, and treating new endeavours like experiments – where there is no answer – but various approaches can be tested, and outcomes reviewed against goals.

A mindset for creativity and innovation

In a shareholder letter in 1997, Jeff Bezos detailed his belief that innovation and failure are inseparable twins.[14] As Edison demonstrated a century before Bezos published this letter, invention is about experimentation, and with that process inevitably comes failure. According to Bezos, this is something most large organizations can't stomach – to put it simply, organizations want to reap the rewards of innovation, but they don't necessarily have the risk appetite to justify the failure that may ensue in the process. Bezos' view is that large returns often occur when you bet against the norm – which is risky as convention often turns out to be right. Sticking with tried and tested methods is unlikely to push knowledge, products, services or society forward – and it's these big pushes into the unknown that can create huge results.

Sticking with tried and tested methods is unlikely to push knowledge, products, services or society forward – and it's these big pushes into the unknown that can create huge results.

Pixar Animation Studios is the home to incredibly talented animators who have created ground-breaking animation productions such as *Toy Story*, *Monsters Inc*, *Finding Nemo*, *The Incredibles* and *Cars*. In the book *Creativity Inc.*, Ed Catmull, co-founder of Pixar, describes how key principles have cemented innovation at the heart of the culture of the organization.[15] Catmull explains how experience has taught him that trying to avoid failing comes at a cost that's often greater than the cost of fixing the mistake. In essence, not moving ideas and actions in new, unproven and unknown directions in the long run stifles innovation. It's more effective to try new ideas and learn from the process than avoid novel new approaches for fear of how failure will be perceived. Because of this belief, Catmull has created an organization where failure isn't viewed as negative – by the leadership team, managers and even team members – rather failure is discussed openly and embraced collectively as an experience the whole team can learn from to move projects forward.

This isn't easy to achieve. Employees at Pixar have had to challenge their own perspectives at times, deal with bruised egos and learn to be open about the experience of making mistakes. There have also been many occasions where projects haven't been delivered on time, or huge parts of a project have been scrapped, because rather than continue a path that won't achieve the best results, animators and their teams are empowered to make the difficult call to start over, or go in a different direction, regardless of the impact on time or budget. This is one of the reasons organizational cultures don't always fully support failure – it can be costly, and can push agreed delivery schedules. Executives at Pixar, however, understand that failure is the cost of doing something exceptional.[16]

Innovation isn't just about failure, however. Sometimes it's about taking a risk and forging a new path. Kikkoman soy sauce was founded in 1917, when eight soy sauce makers who since the 17th century had operated in the same town collectively agreed that rather than competing against each other, they could work together to build a much stronger brand and take hold of a proportionately larger share of the market. These companies pooled their knowledge and facilities, in the process creating a company that is still one of the most well-known products sold today.

It takes a growth mindset to understand the impact of merging knowledge and ideas, rather than competing. This is rarely a painless process, but the rewards of weighing up the options when considering growth and taking bold steps can pay off. Kikkoman's story continues with a growth mindset theme with the approach taken to gain foothold in new markets. Rather than trying to convince customers who probably hadn't come across soy sauce before of the virtues of the product, and attempt to encourage them to pair soy sauce with perhaps unfamiliar Asian foods, customers were encouraged to incorporate soy sauce into dishes that were familiar to them. This proved to be a much easier sell to new customers who weren't necessarily familiar with Asian cuisine. This seems like a genius approach today, and the most logical option at the time would most likely have been to convince customers to broaden their tastes to incorporate a whole new cuisine. Yet, focusing on the desired outcome – which was building interest in bottles of soy sauce to a new market – rather than focusing on one possible logical step – convincing people to use soy sauce in the way it was traditionally used – demonstrates broad, flexible and open thinking, which are all components of a growth mindset.

It takes a growth mindset to understand the impact of merging knowledge and ideas, rather than competing.

Psychological safety

Pixar Animation Studios showcases a culture where failure is embraced, and team members feel safe and empowered to take risks. In fact, managers are explicitly advised it isn't their job to prevent risk, which is a sentiment that has been replicated in few organizations in the past. Traditionally, a risk-adverse attitude has been perceived as the safe approach – a way to keep the business chugging along. As Jeff Bezos alluded to, taking a risk can be costly; in fact, most times it *is* costly. The payoffs, however, can be huge. In today's ever-changing workplace, we don't have the option to play it safe, do things the way they've always been done and avoid calculated risks.

There are two reasons this strategy won't work today. The world is changing around us at a speed we've not encountered for decades. If we don't respond, we will get left behind. Businesses will fail. Employees will find their skills obsolete. Second, the digital and technological landscape is evolving so quickly, if we choose not to keep up, we'll fall behind competitors who are investing in that development. Whether you're running a business or navigating your own career, these things matter.

With every choice there is a trade-off

If we need to adapt to the environment, to some extent we need to take risks. Where do you invest your energy when it comes to learning new skills and honing your knowledge? Where do you decide to invest your time to explore new opportunities, either for yourself or your business? And where do you invest your budget to make innovation a priority?

With every choice there is a trade-off, the things you can't do. Maybe it's choosing one project over another or focusing on developing one product over another. Perhaps it's spending every spare hour you have studying and learning to take your career in the direction you want it to go, and forsaking rest for a period of time. With every new direction you take, there is the chance it may not go to plan; it's likely you will make mistakes along the way, perhaps even feel like you've failed.

In today's unpredictable and competitive work environment, the ability for managers to create psychological safety is critical. In her book *The Fearless Organization*, Amy Edmondson explains why you need team members to speak up – to support innovation and to prevent extreme business failures.[17] Let's look at what happens when you have a team that don't feel psychologically safe. People don't ask questions to clarify their understanding, they just try their best to get through what they think is expected of them. They don't raise concerns if they see a near miss where things could have gone seriously wrong, or when they notice a change in what competitors are offering or clients want. Ultimately, those who don't experience psychological safety at work do their utmost not to make any noise, not stand out either as a problem or as the person highlighting problems, and are less likely to feel empowered to make necessary changes to achieve goals in a complex and uncertain world.

You may be leading a team, in which case one of your main goals needs to be helping your team to feel empowered to speak up, identify risks and take bold steps to overcome challenges. Consider your appetite for risk – do you encourage your teams to take calculated risks to achieve significant rewards? Or does the thought of this kind of approach fill you with dread? Often, leaders feel failure is bad, and assume that correcting mistakes and learning from them is an easy process. However, failure isn't always negative; sometimes it's necessary and changes are made to processes, products and services that end up creating a far more desirable result. Often learning is superficial – think a report on an event, or a team discussion where blame is attributed. The key here is to understand: how does this learning direct future actions? How is the new information used to adjust future processes?

If you're working in a team where you don't feel that you can openly discuss challenges and mistakes, and you don't feel like you can be your authentic self, consider whether this is an environment that is going to allow you to flourish in your career. When it comes to psychological safety, leaders must create the conditions, but team members need to make the sometimes-difficult decisions to admit when mistakes have occurred, highlight challenges and take accountability when the opportunities have been created to do so. If you feel that you don't work within these conditions, and you're fearful of getting things wrong, discussing risks or appearing inept if you don't have all the answers, consider whether you're in the right role for you. As unpredictability and complexity continue to shape the working environment, psychological safety at work will become a non-negotiable requirement.

psychological safety and work will become a non-negotiable requirement

A thriving mindset

As explored so far, how you think, perceive the world and frame experiences can impact how you tackle change, uncertainty and a complex working environment. Nurturing a growth mindset reinforces the belief that positive attributes, skills and intelligence are malleable and can be developed, helping to shape a positive and healthy response to stressful situations, whereby individuals focus on using and developing personal strategies that act as tools to navigate change.[18] A growth mindset also supports psychological resilience, and building resilience reserves can help to prepare you for challenges that may occur in the workplace[19] and buffer against future stress, which is important as challenges start to come at us at a faster pace than ever before. In the next coaching chapter I'll share tips, tools and strategies to help you develop and nurture a growth mindset.

CHAPTER 07

Coaching: Learning forward

What do people who consistently perform at their peak have in common? It's not a specific ability or skill. It's not even knowledge. It's a growth mindset. Whether you want to push the boundaries of your current abilities to achieve more, inspire and lead others to create success, or learn to thrive in challenging situations, a growth mindset is your fuel. In this coaching chapter, you'll have the opportunity to put exercises and strategies to use to help you nurture a growth mindset.

As we explored in the last chapter, success in almost every area of your life can be influenced by how you think about talents and abilities. If you have a growth mindset you believe abilities and skills can change over time; learning and achieving more is in your control and can happen with focused practice. On the flip side, if you have a fixed mindset, you believe your skills and abilities won't or can't change too much over time; you have a level of talent you're born with, which you have very little control over. You may find yourself somewhere in between, whereby sometimes you lead with a growth mindset, and at other times with a fixed mindset.

◎ MINDSET IDENTIFIER EXERCISE
Although you may be prone to using a fixed or growth mindset, many people use a mindset somewhere in between – so, sometimes fixed, sometimes growth. You might find that in general you have a mindset preference. Perhaps you're always looking to learn more, and you learn from challenging experiences with a growth mindset. Or maybe you generally have a fixed mindset and feel that success comes from talent, or your abilities cannot be changed too much over time.

You may even be somewhere in between. For example, I would consider myself as someone who purposely uses a mixed mindset. You may be surprised to read this as I talk about a growth mindset in my work, but the key point for me is to use a growth mindset where it *makes sense* and *matters* to me. I'm not great at any kind of sport, it's never been my forte or of interest to me. So, I don't put my energy into stretching my sporting abilities. In the gym, however, I put huge amounts of effort into getting better and learning more, and that's because it's an activity that I enjoy and that's important to me, so that's where I place my energy when it comes to stretching my physical abilities.

A deliberate mixed mindset is one thing, but you may also experience an unconscious fixed mindset at times, and this is something I can also identify with. At times, I find my role as a parent overwhelming and ambiguous. I'm learning that it's impossible to know if you're making the right decisions at every new stage, and I make mistakes. Although at times I think with a growth mindset and appreciate the fact I'm learning, and I'm tweaking my approach to parenting, all the time trying to become better at my role as a parent, at other times I have a fixed mindset where I feel overwhelmed and destined to be and remain a terrible parent. And yet, in my working life, I have nothing but a growth mindset – I believe I can achieve all the goals I set for myself.

The fact you can have a different mindset in different areas of your life can make it hard to identify whether you have a growth, fixed or mixed mindset. In my opinion, however, categorizing yourself isn't particularly useful. What happens if you find out that you generally have a growth mindset? How do you use that information? Do you continue to nurture that mindset? Do you even need to? I think it's far more effective (and interesting) to understand in which *particular* circumstances you have a specific mindset and work with that. For example, you may generally have a growth mindset at work, but there are some situations that challenge this for you. You can do something productive with that information – you can hone in on the events where you slip into a mixed or fixed mindset and work towards a growth mindset in these situations (which we'll explore later in this chapter).

Take some time to consider areas of your life where you may have a growth, fixed or mixed mindset. Use the template in Table 7.1 for one area of your life, so in this case it could be work (you could also use this exercise focusing on relationships, parenting, hobbies, etc). Consider where your mindset is in different areas – so you may feel like you have a growth mindset when it comes to working on product development or leading project teams – you keep learning and developing your skills to achieve a better result. But you have a fixed mindset when it comes to presenting in front of others, or in feedback meetings – at times you feel like you'll never master the skills you need in these situations.

You may find you have a fixed mindset in some areas of your working life, and this may suit you, just as I described I don't focus on trying to develop my sporting abilities. Or you may find your mindset in these areas is holding you back – maybe you have a fixed mindset about presenting information and you feel you'll never get better, but you need to master this skill to progress in your career.

The first step in this exercise is identifying where you may have a fixed mindset. You can use the template in Table 7.1 to help with this. The second step is deciding how you feel about that – are you satisfied with a fixed mindset in this area, or is it holding you back? So imagine you've had some feedback to say you could do with improving your presentation skills. If you need to be able to present effectively in front of clients to take the next step in your career – which is a role you desperately want – you would probably want to take a growth mindset

TABLE 7.1   Mindset identifier template

Mindset at work

Growth mindset activities

Note the situations in which you feel:

- if you work at it, you can increase your skills and ability
- you can always improve, even by small steps
- even if you don't have natural talent, you can still work to be talented
- learning new skills is in your control

Fixed mindset activities

Note the situations in which you feel:

- you can't change your ability level
- your abilities won't change too much over time
- you don't have natural talent, and there isn't much you can do to change that
- it's hard to keep learning new skills and you can't always control this

Activities

-
-
-

Activities

-
-
-

Situations where I'd like to develop a new growth mindset

-
-
-

Reasons this is important

-
-

approach and tell yourself you can learn to develop these skills. On the flip side, if you have no desire to use presentation skills in your role, and you're thinking of a career change anyway, maybe you don't need a growth mindset when thinking about developing these skills – you might decide it's fine to think you can't really improve these skills (much like my sport example).

Finally, if you want to make changes to stretch your mindset towards growth, you can identify situations where you want to make this happen. In reality, you need a growth mindset for skills that you want to develop in your future career, otherwise you'll get left behind as the competitive world of work evolves. The key is to be strategic about where you place your growth energy. The rest of the exercises in this chapter can help you to develop your mindset in those areas you want to focus on.

◎ CONTINUOUS IMPROVEMENT EXERCISE

Part of nurturing a growth mindset is acknowledging the fact that your learning path is never complete. There is always more to learn and other ways you can push the boundaries of your knowledge and skills. Even if you're an expert in your field, the world is changing, new advances will be made in your area of expertise, or new information discovered, all of which can negatively impact your level of expertise if you don't focus on staying informed.

Learning how to create a continuous development outlook will help you to hone your growth mindset. The idea is to create a process whereby you expand your knowledge, broaden your skills, test new approaches, review progress and make tweaks to enhance your performance in the future. By viewing this as a process, almost like a scientific experiment, it helps take the emotion out of it when things don't go to plan. This provides you with the opportunity to objectively view your efforts as an experiment, and it can reduce the stigma and emotional response we often associate with making mistakes or even failing.

This exercise is based on 'kaizen' methodology, which is a Japanese process that refers to continuous improvement across all business functions in the workplace.[1] You can apply the kaizen principles to your life and career by focusing on small ways you can make improvements or changes in order to keep progressing and moving forward effectively in your career. By adopting this practice and routine, you're not only future-proofing your career; you're also creating a habit that will serve you well in challenging and unpredictable circumstances. If you get used to the concept of making small tweaks to practices and processes, when you're forced to make changes and adjust to new expectations you'll have a process you can use to guide you.

The next time you plan to expand your knowledge and put what you've learned into practice, take some time to create your own test experiment process. Get really clear on what you're testing and think about answering these questions:

- What skills are you developing?
- What knowledge are you putting into action?
- Why this is important for you?
- What do you hope to achieve?

Next, set a continuous development process, which has three steps:

Review → Refine → Repeat

This is a very simple exercise, and can be used frequently; I recommend a weekly review (Table 7.2 may help). Take

TABLE 7.2 Continuous improvement template

Review	Refine
What went well	Changes I'll make next week
◉	◉
What didn't go so well	◉
◉	◉
What I learned	◉
◉	◉
Where my focus needs to be in future	◉
◉	◉

Repeat
Next review date
◉

some time, maybe 20 minutes, to review the week. Note down what went well, what didn't go so well, what you learned, and where your focus needs to be over the coming week. Try to be as objective as possible. Celebrate the successes, but also celebrate the fact you've tried to progress, even if things don't go to plan.

Next, focus on what you need to refine – this is about making small tweaks to the way you do things, streamlining a process, or gathering more information to help you move forward with your projects and goals. What tweaks could you make? What did you learn in the process that will help you to achieve a better result in the future? What won't you try again, because it just didn't work that well?

Finally, repeat this process, again and again, ideally by making it a habit. It's the repetition part which creates a habit and will help you to recognize when change is needed and adapt to new conditions. Consider how you'll commit to continuing this process. Do you need to block out time in your diary? Do you need someone to hold you accountable?

Understanding things won't always go to plan, creating a strong review process, and treating your growth and development as a scientific experiment will help you to develop a successful growth mindset. It will also set you up on the path of lifelong learning, helping you to turn challenges into opportunities to learn.

◎ BELIEF EXERCISE

Sometimes we find it easier to believe in the abilities of others more than we believe in ourselves. This exercise will help you tap into the belief that people can choose to learn, develop and achieve more, and over time you can apply this perspective to yourself.

Consider a time when someone you care about doubted their ability to achieve something. Write an encouraging message to this person, explaining why you think they have the ability to reach their goals. Highlight the evidence you have to support your belief in them, and how you've seen them overcome challenges in the past. In your note cover these areas:

- Why you believe in them
- Evidence you have to support your belief in them (why you *know* they can achieve what they've set out to do)
- How they've overcome challenges in the past

This is a wonderful exercise as it helps you to appreciate others and be part of a support system for others (which, as we covered in Chapter 2, is an important part of building resilience).

The next step in this exercise is to link this back to your own mindset. How does this exercise make you feel about challenges you face? Could you create an encouraging message to yourself? When you face obstacles, could you change the way you talk to yourself, perhaps in a more supportive and encouraging tone, like you would a friend?

Adopting a growth mindset with others can at times be easier than applying the same mindset to our own lives. Start to reframe your thinking to help others focus on developing a growth mindset, and then work on transferring this way of thinking to yourself and your own life.

◉ ADD 'YET' TO YOUR STORY EXERCISE

Part of building a growth mindset is understanding you're on a learning journey – there are always ways you can develop further and expand on your skills and knowledge. This journey is even more changeable and complex in today's working environment. We're all navigating new developments in how and why we work, at a pace we've never experienced before. This means we can't possibly always have the answers about how to navigate change effectively because as a global society we've not seen these changes previously. We must learn as we go, which involves some trial and error at times.

When the stakes are high and you're operating in a complex, fast-paced and unpredictable working environment, it can be hard not to feel deflated, frustrated or even angry when you've made a mistake, or the project you're working on hasn't gone to plan. These feelings are valid and shouldn't be avoided – this is often part of the messy middle when you're developing or creating something new – whether that be a product, process or team. It's not the part of the story where you're motivated to get going at the start, or the end where you've achieved something of value. It's the tricky part in the middle where it doesn't always go to plan.

There is, however, a simple way you can change the way you view these situations – by adding the simple word 'yet' to the end of a sentence when you think and talk about your progress. Here's an example of how you can change your thinking:

Thought: I didn't get funding for my project.

↓

Altered to: I haven't managed to secure funding *yet*.

Whichever disappointing situation you're thinking of, is there a way to add the word 'yet' to the end of the sentence? So – I haven't found a solution...*yet*, or I haven't passed the bar exam... *yet*, or I haven't secured a promotion... *yet*.

This way, you start to frame events as work in progress, a story where you haven't yet reached the end. Imagine you were writing a book about your progress. If you were to stop at a failure, that's your last chapter. But if you continue to write the story, you could have a whole lot more success in front of you. By adding the 'yet' you're not finishing your story too soon, and you're indicating to yourself and others you're still working on finding a solution, and where you are right now could just be the messy middle.

◎ FAILING FORWARD EXERCISE

Part of any kind of growth is about pushing past barriers and entering uncharted territory. Failure is unavoidable, and in fact is a very important part of life. In our professional lives we are guaranteed to experience at least a few failures, whether big or small. We need to learn to harness failure and use it to our advantage instead of letting it hold us back.

Central to this is reducing the stigma of failing, and instead focusing on the end goal. People are often scared of things not working out due to subsequent feelings of shame, embarrassment and guilt, so avoid taking risks or trying a different approach. In order to really accept and celebrate failure, you need to develop cognitive flexibility – reframing difficult situations, thoughts and emotions to view them as a rich part of life and work (exercises in Chapter 5 can also help you to develop cognitive flexibility).

Those who use failure to fuel success understand that both opportunities and obstacles will present themselves, and that's normal; failing at something doesn't have to be a negative experience, it can just be a sign that there's a need to move in a different direction, try something new, or keep practising a skill. When you realize that most successes are built on the experience of many failures, you can begin to see them as not failures at all, but an essential part of the process and crucial to being able to grow and develop in your career.

The good news is you can turn mistakes, failure and challenges to your advantage. It's all about adjusting your perspective to see events that don't go to plan as part of the process of learning and developing. The key is to prepare yourself for potential challenges and accept that you may fail as you start to put new ideas and skills into practice. You also need to understand that making decisions that don't always pay off is just a normal part of the process. In fact, rather than just accepting mistakes may occur, if you can learn to celebrate failure, you'll create a way of thinking that helps you to thrive.

Here are three ways you can turn mistakes and failure into learning experiences:

- **Create a failure wall**. Document all your efforts that haven't been fruitful or created the results you wanted. Maybe your project budget was pulled, an interview didn't go as planned, you didn't get the promotion, a presentation didn't go well, or you didn't receive funding. These are painful experiences potentially but looking at the work you've put in will help you to appreciate your effort. A failure in one area may turn out to be a success in another project in the future. Also, documenting how many failures it takes to create success will help you to view mistakes and challenges as part of the process of creating successful outcomes.

- **Change the 'win–lose' language**. We often look at events in life as binary – we win, or we lose, and these are opposite ends of the scale. But this isn't always reflective of reality. What about if you win a project but lose a relationship in the process? What if you lose out in a client pitch, but you learned so much that will help you with your next pitch? Rather than focusing on winning or success as an outcome, shift your thinking to celebrate the process of getting to where you are, celebrate the effort, energy, motivation, creativity and resourcefulness you demonstrated. If you can learn to value the process rather than just the outcome, you can take positives from the situation, even when you don't achieve what you set out to.

- **Share your failures in real time**. Sometimes when you look back, you can appreciate how failing eventually helped you on your career journey. Perhaps you learned something important about what to do, or even what not to do. Maybe you changed direction, learned to innovate, worked on your resilience, or built motivation. Perhaps you let go of something that just wasn't working for you. These stories are great to share but doing so as they happen makes a difference. If you can share your experiences at the time with those you trust you can garner support (which, as we explored in Chapter 2, helps to build resilience), and you can help reduce the feelings of embarrassment or shame that others may feel when they make mistakes.

Overall, it's important to celebrate the failures that show you took a leap. Failing forward isn't about toxic positivity and pretending to feel great about a challenging situation or bitter disappointment – this approach can be psychologically damaging over time. You can acknowledge and accept painful feelings you experience with failure and, as you'll see in the next chapter, it's possible to experience challenging emotions and find ways to keep moving forward at the same time.

Failing forward is about learning from the experience, which helps you to grow and develop in the future. Not all failures lead to future success – some mistakes are lessons that teach us what we don't want, or how not to approach a situation. There is, however, *always* something you can learn about the situation or yourself when things don't go to plan.

◎ THE CHALLENGE EXERCISE

A simple way to nurture a growth mindset is to set yourself a goal that's going to stretch and challenge you. Working towards achieving something you haven't done before will push you outside your comfort zone as you learn new skills or acquire new knowledge. Although personal and professional growth can occur through learning that is outside your control (such as a change in processes, new targets being set, a merger and acquisition you're part of), you can also take control to direct your learning and development, and in the process stretch your abilities and nurture a growth mindset.

When it comes to setting goals that you're motivated to achieve, mental contrasting is an effective goal achievement technique. There are three steps:

1 Envisioning what the future will look like when you reach a goal that's important to you.
2 Thinking about the reality of where you are right now, which isn't as desirable as your future goal.
3 Reflecting on the contrast between your current reality and future goal.

The contrasting between now and the future can help you to consider how you will tackle challenges that threaten goal achievement before those potential obstacles materialize. This is useful to do before challenges arise, because in the moment it's often hard to find time to think about how to tackle a challenge, willpower can be lower, and it can be difficult to stay motivated to keep pursuing goals when the going gets tough. The idea is you think through how you will overcome potential obstacles ahead of time, so you're ready to deal with them when they actually occur. Also, the action of contrasting can be motivating, as you consider what you want to leave behind in your current reality and what you want to achieve in your future.

You can challenge yourself to set a goal right now, and work through the first step in this process – think deeply about what your future will look like when you reach the goal. Compare that to your reality right now and consider how your life will change. I recommend checking in on progress frequently, maybe in a monthly review. Think about your goal progress and challenges you've faced. If you're finding it hard to take action to reach your goal or overcome obstacles, again compare your future to today and remind yourself of what you're working towards, and most importantly why you're working towards it. This will help you to find a way to learn and grow to reach the goals you've set out for yourself, and in the process develop your growth mindset.

The exercises in this chapter will help you to believe you can work towards goals that matter to you, you can learn more and achieve more, and you can find the psychological resources to navigate change and overcome challenges. In the next chapter, we'll look at how to use a growth mindset to build another critical skill in the workplace today – emotional intelligence.

CHAPTER 08

Emotional intelligence

When it comes to dealing with uncertainty and finding a way to thrive when the world is complicated and uncertain, it's essential to build emotional intelligence. Unlike the measure of general intelligence – the intelligence quotient (or IQ) – which is fairly fixed and stable over time, emotional intelligence can change and be developed. Although the idea of emotional intelligence can seem complicated, at its root are simple concepts: understanding and expressing emotions and being empathetic when communicating with others.

Emotional intelligence at work has been a hot topic for the past decade, and today it's still an issue that executives, leaders and employees want to understand better to achieve results. My LinkedIn Learning course on the topic has been taken by over one million learners, and regularly makes the top course lists.[1] It seems that people are eager to learn more about the concept of emotional intelligence and understand how to apply the skills to their working lives.

How did emotional intelligence become such a hot topic at work? In part, this is because the impact of emotional intelligence is backed by research, which tells us it can support collaboration across teams and promote innovation.[2] High levels of emotional intelligence have also been linked to lower levels of stress and better psychological and physical health. Those who have higher levels of emotional intelligence display better decision-making skills when under pressure, and higher levels of performance when compared with those who have lower levels of emotional intelligence.

The rise of the focus on emotional intelligence at work is also in part because the concept is accessible and easy to apply – in our busy working lives we want simple and effective tools that can help us to thrive at work. It's important, however, to use an evidence-based approach when building emotional intelligence, which is exactly what we'll explore in this chapter and the next coaching chapter.

The emotions in emotional intelligence

Emotions are complex. According to Lisa Feldman Barrett in her book *How Emotions Are Made*, emotions are psychological experiences that we construct based on our personal history, experiences and physiology.[3] Emotions are an insight into how we interpret events around us, and how we feel about these events. They can reflect pleasure or displeasure and can be extreme or mild. If you've felt intense anger, happiness or joy, that's a psychological state influenced in part by your emotions. When it comes to experiencing emotions, there's so much room for variation between each of us – you may react to the exact same situation in a completely different way to me. There's also the potential for variation *within* us. Have you ever reacted to an event in an extreme way, when you know on another day it would have just been a mild irritation for you?

much of how we perceive and interact with the world around us can be derived from our emotions

Understanding and managing your emotions is critical if you want to enhance your performance and interact successfully with others, because much of how we perceive and interact with the world around us can be derived from our emotions. And if we're not consciously managing this process, our emotions are taking the lead. At times, this may work in our favour, but it also may not, which is why being conscious of this process is a crucial step when it comes to managing behaviour and relationships with others at work.

Today, many of us work within changeable and pressured environments, which can heighten emotions we experience, and fuel our reactions to events. One of the workplace challenges I've been working on with coaching clients recently is creating strategies to build strong relationships in an increasingly uncertain environment. For those that work in organizations where they're not always physically located with their team, the opportunity for informal connections has been negatively impacted – we miss opportunities to chat over coffee, walk to a meeting together and discuss a project, bump into a colleague you haven't seen in a while and take the opportunity to check in. The opportunity for social learning has also become less frequent; we can learn a lot about culture, workplace politics and personalities from taking in what's going on in a social situation.

With fewer opportunities to informally build relationships, challenging conversations can be harder to navigate. You may have experienced this – you need to negotiate with a colleague or client and you're trying to pick up on social cues through a screen. Or you need to deliver some challenging news to a colleague, and it feels more formal having to book a time to connect virtually rather than being able to deliver the news face to face. Consider those that have started new roles and haven't had to navigate building relationships virtually before. Of course, some people have always worked remotely and have strategies to navigate these situations already in place, but this is uncharted territory for many people. It's not so much the situation that can affect our emotions – we all have different challenges we're navigating – it's more the change we're experiencing that affects how we feel about our working lives. For some, that change could be a new role, a new working location or a promotion.

Part of the process of dealing with uncertainty is navigating the feelings that accompany the change. You may feel excited, hopeful, overwhelmed, anxious or nervous – or a mix of all of these. You might find you also experience physiological responses to these emotions, like a surge of energy when you feel excited, or sweating palms when you feel nervous. Emotions are core to who we are, and they provide us with a rich way to experience life. However, they don't always serve us in our best interest, so it's important to understand our emotions and how they affect our relationships with others at work.

The concept of emotional intelligence

In a challenging situation at work, when you experience intense emotions that aren't always positive, it can impact how you interact with others. Building emotional intelligence can help to make the process of dealing with change less overwhelming, and more positive.

Although the concept of emotional intelligence differs slightly in varying research papers, one of the most effective and easiest models to apply is that outlined by Daniel Goleman in his book *Emotional Intelligence*.[4] There are four areas of emotional intelligence:

- self-awareness
- self-management
- social awareness
- relationship management or development

What you'll notice is the first two parts look inwards, focusing on yourself, by understanding and learning to manage your emotions. The second two parts are outward facing, focusing on building awareness in social situations and managing and developing relationships.

Self-awareness

Have you ever been in a situation where someone else's behaviour has made you react strongly? Maybe you've had a difficult exchange with someone at work, and the interaction has made your blood boil and you've lost your temper. The chances are, we can all recount numerous situations where someone else's behaviour has made us react passionately to the situation. The truth of it is, however, it isn't the other person's behaviour that's making us react, although it certainly feels that way in the moment. It's how we think about the situation that leads to a reaction.

Often, we consider our behaviour as a response to an event or something that's happened to us. We tend to think of our own behaviour, and that of others as a reaction to an event that is often out of our control. But there's a step missing in this process. In reality, the chain reaction we experience goes something like this:

An event takes place.

↓

You experience thoughts and emotions relating to the event.

↓

You behave in a way that reflects your thoughts about the situation.

The key here is to understand it isn't the event itself that causes a reaction, and it isn't another person's behaviour. It's how you think and feel about a situation which will lead to your response. This is why sometimes you may be in a situation that leaves you feeling irritated, but at other times when you face a similar situation you'll feel livid. I always use the example of driving – why is it at times when someone cuts me up when I'm driving, I can brush it off, and at others I find myself feeling like my blood is boiling? The difference is the emotional response.

Consider a time when a challenging conversation you've had with a colleague at work has left you feeling angry. What was it about the situation that made you feel that way? Was it the particular person who you have history with, and you expect a difficult exchange whenever you have these conversations? Did something the other person said tap into something that really bothers you and is a trigger for you to become angry? Was it nothing to do with the person, but you were experiencing personal challenges and a really bad day?

Andrea Jung, the chair and CEO of Avon Products, has stated that emotional intelligence, and focusing on self-awareness in particular, is at the heart of the company.[5] As Jung explains, without self-awareness you can't be clear about the impact you have on others. Jung is so focused on self-awareness, she's created a CEO advisory panel whereby ten people chosen from Avon offices around the world provide feedback on positive and challenging situations. Jung knows that, at her level of seniority, very few people are willing to provide candid feedback, so she's created a system whereby she hears what people really think and is prompted to consider how her actions impact others.

Emotional intelligence is in the DNA of Avon culture, an organization where the relationship between the 4.5 million independent sales representatives and their customers is critical to the survival of the business. Emotional intelligence is such an important focus at Avon that training is at the core of its education programme and emotional intelligence is included as a competency in the performance rating process.

Our thoughts and emotions are so powerful, they dictate how we experience the world around us and how we feel about situations. The thinking process can affect how we behave, how we interact with others, the choices and decisions we make and how we perform at work. This process isn't always the slick, well-oiled machine it could be if we want to get the most out of a situation. Your brain can process 11 million pieces of information per second; only 40 to 50 bits are processed in our conscious thinking.[6] Most of the information your brain is processing is subconscious. This is a huge cognitive load, which our brains are designed to handle partly by creating cognitive shortcuts, so information can be processed effectively and quickly without you having to consciously think about it. This protects you from feeling overwhelmed and finding the simplest of decisions a crippling challenge.

Sometimes, however, our automatic information processing doesn't always serve us well. In situations where we fly off the handle and the trigger is something that in hindsight didn't warrant that reaction, it can be useful to slow our reaction down, or have strategies in place to change the automatic process. The first step in emotional intelligence is understanding the emotion – which can take some reflection. I'll share exercises to help with this in the next chapter. It's also helpful to understand why you reacted in the way that you did. Once you start to understand this process, the next stage of building emotional intelligence is managing your emotions and behaviour.

Self-management

Have you ever had that pang of regret when you look back at a situation and feel like you could have handled it better? I certainly have. Reacting quickly in the heat of the moment happens at times to all of us, but what we often don't realize is that we can slow the reaction process down.

Imagine you're finding one of your colleagues particularly challenging lately. You're working on a project with this colleague, and you need them to provide you with information every week, which they are consistently late with. This makes your job so much harder as you need to chase the information and you don't have enough time to collate the data sent through. Today, the colleague ignores your request for the data you need, even though you've pointed out why it's important you receive the information on time. You then start to ruminate on the situation, thinking your colleague doesn't respect you, and they don't believe your work is valid or important. These thoughts lead to you experiencing anger. You pick up the phone and lash out at your colleague in an aggressive manner.

In hindsight, you may reflect and think you could have responded in a more effective way. In emotional intelligence terms, you may start to focus on managing your emotions in a different way once you become aware of them. If you could rewind this event, at the point in time where you felt you weren't being respected, and your colleague was being dismissive, thoughtless or intentionally obstructive, if you can learn to slow your thinking process and challenge your thoughts, you give yourself a good shot at managing your emotions. I'll delve into some tips on how to do this in the next coaching chapter.

With a bit more time to challenge your thoughts, you can start to imagine the situation from the viewpoint of an objective observer. This makes the situation less personal; you can only comment on the facts you see before you. Your colleague is late with the information again – that is the objective and factual analysis of the situation. You can stop your train of thought before assuming your colleague's behaviour reflects how they view you; it may be nothing to do with you. Maybe they're just not clear on how their information affects your work; it may not be an active action, but rather a lack of consideration. This process is about disrupting those initial thoughts that pop into your head, which is a strategy you can use to then choose a different, perhaps more effective, response, which results in you achieving a better outcome. In this case you may decide to meet with your colleague and explain how their work impacts your ability to meet deadlines, and agree a way to work together going forward.

When it comes to managing emotions, it can be useful to understand that we view events from one perspective but there are many more alternative perspectives that we may not have considered. It's also useful to reflect on the fact that there may not be one 'correct' perspective – life is rarely that simple. Instead, there may be various ways a situation can be interpreted, and we will have one view of the possibilities. It can be hard to challenge your own perspective, especially when you feel passionately about a situation. We often assume we see the world in the correct way, and other people are wrong. But this approach can lead to blind spots.

Learning to challenge your views and assumptions about others and their behaviours broadens your horizons and encourages you to learn how to pre-empt how someone else may view a situation. This will help you to understand how best to deal with a challenging scenario, which is the basis for building strong and collaborative relationships. In order to shift your perspective and view events from different points of view, you need to make it a habit and build the process into how you view events before you make decisions about how to behave. I'll detail some strategies you can try to help achieve this in the next coaching chapter.

Social awareness

Have you ever intuitively felt like you've been in a dangerous situation, or you've walked into a new place and immediately felt at home, like it's your kind of place? How does that happen? The chances are you're sub-consciously processing information you've gathered from your senses to build an intuitive picture of your environment. You're subconsciously using social awareness. If you start to build self-awareness and focus on understanding your own emotions and reactions, you can apply the same skills to build your social awareness, which is focused on learning more about others around you and understanding their perspective and emotions.

It's a logical step-by-step process. The first step is focusing on your own self-awareness with an internal focus, which means looking inward and considering what's going on in your head. Once you've started to master this process, the next step is to develop your social awareness, shifting the focus from internal reflection to an outward external observation, thinking about how you interact with others.

Using your senses can help to build your social awareness. Think about using your senses to build a picture of what is going on around you – what can you hear, see, feel? This helps you to gather information and pay attention to your surroundings – whether that be by noticing facial expressions and body language or hearing nuances in tone of voice. If you ever feel like building social awareness is a challenge for you, this practical approach can be learned and developed by everyone, and over time can support you in feeling more confident in interpreting social interactions.

Once you become comfortable in gathering social information, you can start to piece it together to get an idea of what others may be experiencing, and you can work on understanding the dynamics between people. Often, when we describe people as being intuitive, this is the process we're describing. An important part of this process is taking notice. Quite often, information is available to us, but we're juggling so many demands, priorities, emotions and thoughts that it can take some practice to step outside of ourselves and our own thoughts and immerse ourselves in our surroundings.

As Linda Stone, former vice president of corporate and industry initiatives at Microsoft can attest to, empathy is an important part of building emotional intelligence.[7] Empathizing occurs when you make the effort to imagine yourself in the situation or circumstances of another person (figuratively speaking, you 'put yourself in someone else's shoes'), to try to understand what they are experiencing, which helps to build strong relationships and better connections. Ultimately, empathy is the ability to sense other people's emotions while also being able to imagine what someone else may be thinking or feeling. It's a skill you can learn and develop.

It's important, however, to learn to balance your empathy, as Stone learned. Although empathy is a powerful tool that can be used to connect to others, if over-used it can be psychologically and physically draining for the person displaying empathy. In fact, Stone found that over-empathizing took a physical toll on her as she was given the mandate of rebuilding industry relationships at Microsoft, which required her to repair damaged relationships and actively listen to intense feedback.

Over time, this led to exhaustion as Stone felt like she was absorbing everyone's complaints, and her physical health took a hit. Her sleep was disrupted, her stress levels were at an all-time high, and she gained a significant amount of weight. This situation is a stark reminder of why it's important to set boundaries, even when working in what would seem like a positive manner and incorporating empathy into your working life. Stone did start to focus on her health and found a way to use her empathy to create solutions. Rather than absorbing all the issues she was hearing about, she started connecting people who needed to work together to solve issues, in turn, helping them to use empathy. Empathy doesn't have to mean using all your energy to absorb how others feel, rather it's about understanding perspectives and emotions, and establishing healthy boundaries so you can use that information to build strong connections without feeling overwhelmed.

Relationship management

Collaboration at work can be tricky at the best of times, and even more so in an uncertain and changeable environment when it's unclear how your priorities will change, and perhaps even less clear what the priorities of others will be in the future. Working together towards common goals and trying to find common ground is a tricky daily reality for teams. Collaboration is a critical factor in leveraging team effectiveness, and research has found emotional intelligence to be a predictor of collaboration.[8]

Ultimately, effective relationship management is at the heart of collaboration. How is it that some people manage relationships with ease, while some of us are not quite sure where to start? The chances are, for those that naturally manage relationships well, this is a strength that's been developed over time. If managing relationships effectively isn't your forte, or you find it challenging in your current working environment, don't give up on developing this skill. I'll outline some strategies to help in the next chapter. The key is to understand what your unique relationship skills are, and focus on utilizing your own communication style, one that you're comfortable with, when it's in your control to do so. The benefit of finding your own way to manage relationships and communicate is that other people will feel they're making a genuine and authentic connection with you, which will help you to build trust and strong relationships with team members.

How we communicate with others matters when it comes to building relationships. Have you ever experienced a moment where you realized how you intended to come across to someone else had been completely misinterpreted? It can create a feeling of embarrassment, shame or guilt. All too often, we focus on finding the exact, correct words to say, but the impact we make is more about how someone else perceives us and our message, and less about the facts we want other people to grasp. You may have heard the phrase people forget what you say, but they remember how you made them feel. This is true to an extent – people remember some words (especially if the words are shocking, exciting or novel), but mostly people remember the interaction overall.

When building relationships, you can focus on your intention – what you would like to get out of the situation, how you would like the other person to feel – rather than the exact words you want to use (unless you're in a situation, such as a legal encounter, where exact wording is crucial). This can also boost your confidence when communicating, as rather than trying to remember exactly what to say, you instead concentrate on letting the words take care of themselves while you stay focused on why your message is important for the other person. It feels less like an exam where you feel pressurized to get things right, and more like an interaction that you can adapt.

Consider the example of a marketing manager leading a project team. There will be key messages everyone has to know – such as deliverables, key targets and project dependencies. Some of this information must be documented for clarity, but most messages that are delivered to the team are done so informally. One marketing manager may respond best to a one-to-one briefing, whereas you might build a stronger relationship with another with an informal check-in over coffee, or through an email exchange. The key is being able to adapt to the communication style of the individual, and to be adaptable in how you deliver messages.

If you can be agile in your communication – responding to the other person and focusing on the intent behind your words, even if the delivery isn't quite right, the other person is much more likely to listen and engage with you, and you have a greater chance of building trust, which is one of the cornerstones of building strong relationships. You'll also come across as authentic, which is a key factor at play when it comes to connecting with others. The key is to consider the other person's perspective and how they may perceive you.

The only way to truly understand how others perceive you is to is to gather feedback, which can be challenging; sometimes it's more comfortable to live in a bubble, not asking how others see you. The reality is, however, that gathering feedback on how you're coming across to others is one of the most useful techniques you can use to help you build long-term relationships.

When provided with feedback from others, it can at times feel personal, and that can result in an emotional reaction, which is in part why it's so important to tackle the inward-facing parts of emotional intelligence first – self-awareness and self-management – so you have the tools to deal with potentially developmental feedback in an effective way. Gathering feedback is one of the most useful techniques you can use to help you develop professionally and personally. It can help to develop the skills you need to appreciate other points of view without being overly self-critical or defensive. In the next coaching chapter, I'll share strategies to help you receive and deliver feedback effectively.

Leading with emotional intelligence

Leaders today are looking to equip their teams with emotional intelligence, and those that do this well lead by example. Colleen Barrett, COO of Southwest Airlines, believes her intuition and emotional intelligence help her be a good leader. She can read people and pick up on social cues to understand the mood of a group. Barrett believes being attuned to her employees helps her ensure they do their best work. Interestingly, Barrett believes this type of awareness is something that can be developed with experience and learning to observe closely – she listens to everything, pays attention to body language, and watches how people interact.

Emotional intelligence is about being aware of emotions and being conscious of how these emotions are expressed. This requires self-awareness and self-management. Emotional intelligence isn't only an inward-facing tool; part of building emotional intelligence is developing social awareness and managing and developing relationships with others effectively. Barrett uses the outward-facing facets of emotional intelligence to understand others and the context around her – building social awareness. She also takes an individual approach to building relationships, adapting her style depending on how best the other person will respond.

The aim of building emotional intelligence isn't to get it 'right'. Rather, it's about developing awareness, both personal and social, to build strong connections with others, interacting with individuals in the most effective way. Barrett is self-aware and knows being an emotional leader sometimes causes her to communicate in passionate ways that aren't always well received and can sometimes lead to her ideas and contributions being disregarded – particularly, she says, as a woman in a predominantly male environment. She has learned to surround herself with people who can temper her and flag when her arguments could be communicated in a more effective way. Her emotions lead her to great ideas and conclusions – however, she knows that to get her point across she needs to prepare what she is going to say so the message can be delivered in a calm, logical way with facts to back her up. Social aware-ness isn't only about understanding others and what's going on around you, it's also about adapting your approach to a situation to achieve results – such as having a trusted team around you with strengths that complement your own.

When leading others, it's important to understand and accept different ways of managing and expressing emotions. In fact, this is a core component of leading with emotional intelligence. Whether you're leading teams, projects or yourself, role modelling by working on the four areas of emotional intelligence will show others around you how to build their emotional intelligence to improve performance and relationships. Research suggests that leading with emotional intelligence can support positive behaviours across the organization, so it isn't just the leader and their teams that benefit, but there's the opportunity to build a culture of positive behaviour that affects the wider organization.[9]

The entrepreneur Richard Branson is a great example of someone who leads with emotional intelligence. Branson's philosophy at Virgin is to empower people to be exceptional leaders, who care about what their employees think and feel – these leaders need to be self-aware and socially aware. They need to consider how they manage their emotions in complex and heated moments at work, and they need to build strong connections. Branson believes a business will only be successful if its people are enthusiastic and passionate. He makes recognition and fun key components of all Virgin businesses and ensures his leadership team make sure individual needs don't lose out to the wider vision – a principle he also personally practices.

Constructive conflict and emotional intelligence

Andrea Jung, the CEO of Avon, describes how she grew up in a household that was averse to conflict, which could have hindered her ability to make tough decisions and have challenging conversations. Jung's working style is naturally more collaborative, which is an essential factor in leveraging team effectiveness. Research has shown that emotional intelligence can support collaboration,[10] so it isn't surprising that Jung, who is focused on emotional intelligence, also feels comfortable using a collaborative communication style.

Interestingly, in Jung's career journey she became aware that collaboration can at times be a barrier to making the tough calls that are part of the job as a senior executive. When delivering bad news and managing conflict, Jung has developed her leadership style to act with compassion and fairness, using empathy to manage these challenging situations. As Jung knows, healthy conflict is an essential component of a healthy business.

As we work in an increasingly innovative and fast-paced environment, we will face conflict of opinions. Whenever a decision needs to be made about what steps to take next to navigate change or remain competitive, people will have varying views based on their priorities, values and objectives. Contrary to logic, perhaps, conflict is a healthy part of interaction within organizations – the key is to make the conflict productive and respectful rather than toxic.

There is a strong body of research to suggest emotional intelligence can support constructive conflict management.

A study carried out in hospitals in Indonesia found emotional intelligence influences team performance by promoting factors such as constructive conflict.[11] This research doesn't prove emotional intelligence causes better conflict management and performance (because of the way the experiment was set up), but it does point to a correlation of some kind between the presence of emotional intelligence, performance and positive conflict management. This is a promising place to start for research into this area to develop in the future.

Another study conducted in the USA found high levels of emotional intelligence to positively correlate with conflict-handling strategies that favour mutual interests – a key component of constructive, healthy and productive conflict.[12] The presence of emotional intelligence also correlated with helpful workplace behaviours, particularly in pressurized and charged situations. Again, cause and effect may not be clear from the study design, but this does provide interesting data to suggest emotional intelligence could help those with opposing opinions to find a way to negotiate in a manner that is beneficial for all parties, which is a skill teams need today more than ever, particularly in stressful situations.

Research suggests that emotional intelligence is a key component in practising positive conflict management behaviours which can be replicated around the world. A study conducted across 79 teams in South Korea found that the presence of team emotional intelligence reduces the chances of conflicts relating to tasks and relationships, and increases team performance and innovation.[13]

Emotional intelligence was in fact found to be a buffer between conflict on the one hand, and team effectiveness or team cohesion on the other.

Although it can be hard to draw conclusions on the impact of emotional intelligence when looking at individual studies, meta-analysis data studies (which combine data from a wide set of studies, creating a much wider data pool) can offer insights into how emotional intelligence impacts individuals and culture at work on a larger scale. Research of this type, which compared and collated data across 20 studies and over 5,000 participants, found emotional intelligence to be positively associated with constructive conflict management.[14] This provides strong evidence to support what we're starting to witness in organizations – we need emotionally intelligent teams to have intelligent debates and navigate inevitable conflict successfully.

Stress and emotional intelligence

Team benefits of emotional intelligence are well reported, as are the benefits research has shown may apply to the individual at work. Perhaps the most well-documented outcome of emotional intelligence is improved psychological wellbeing, and in particular the reduction of stress. A study conducted with Italian school teachers found those that reported themselves to be emotionally intelligent (measured via a valid questionnaire) also reported higher satisfaction and engagement with their work, and lower levels of burnout – which can be described as excessive amounts of prolonged stress.[15]

Interestingly, research has also suggested a relationship between emotional intelligence and effective decision making in pressurized situations. Results from a study which included those that often face stressful emergencies at work, such as doctors, paramedics and police, found when emotional intelligence levels were high, decision-making skills were better in pressurized situations. On the flip side, when emotional intelligence was low, the decisions of those taking part in the study were not as effective in stressful situations.[16] Of course, this is one study and further research in the area would be useful to understand this relationship in more detail. This study does, however, point to promising results, suggesting emotional intelligence can be used to help us all make better decisions when we feel pressurized or stressed, which is particularly relevant to the volatile and uncertain workplace we're all operating in today.

Meta-analysis reveals how, exactly, emotional intelligence helps to reduce stress. A meta-analysis combines and compares data across many studies to find trends, providing a more in-depth view of what research is telling us. A meta-analysis including data from almost 8,000 people found emotional intelligence to be associated with positive mental health.[17]

The evidence supporting the connection between emotional intelligence and better psychological health is extensive and has important implications in the workplace today, where stress is at an all-time high and our working lives have the potential to become more complex. If we can develop emotional intelligence, this could be one way to deal with the effects of stress. Psychological health isn't the only personal outcome associated with emotional intelligence, however; the link between emotional intelligence and performance is also becoming clearer.

Emotional intelligence, learning and performance

A Spanish study that included 1,048 participants found those with high levels of emotional intelligence and low levels of stress showed the highest performance.[18] This is interesting, as we know from research that emotional intelligence behaviours can help to reduce stress. This data suggests emotional intelligence can impact performance also – possibly through the process of reducing stress.

A study that analysed diary entries for over 200 people found that reflecting on the emotions of others increased active learning. In addition, those that reflected on their own emotions were more likely to report higher energy levels.[19] Both learning and high energy are precursors to high performance, so this research draws an interesting link between self-awareness (reflecting on own emotions) and social awareness (understanding the emotions of others) and performance at work.

A meta-analysis has also been conducted in the area of emotional intelligence and performance. This study confirms what smaller samples in research studies tell us – emotional intelligence positively correlates with job performance.[20] This has huge implications for how we manage our personal emotional intelligence at work, suggesting that the skills and behaviours of emotional intelligence are important tools and strategies that we need to learn to improve performance.

Building emotional intelligence at work

The benefits of building emotional intelligence are well documented – the more you use your emotional intelligence, the more likely you are to perform better during times of uncertainty, manage conflict constructively and build strong relationships. You're also less likely to experience stress, and the negative outcomes associated with that. In short, developing emotional intelligence helps you to thrive in uncertainty.

Join me in the next coaching chapter where I'll share tools, strategies and tips you can use to enhance your emotional intelligence.

CHAPTER 09

Coaching:
Interacting with the world

Success in many of today's workplaces relies heavily on teamwork, communication and innovation, which can all be improved significantly through developing emotional intelligence. Applying emotional intelligence at work can also facilitate the capacity to deal with stress and navigate change, thus helping to enhance performance and wellbeing. As the working world continues to evolve, uncertainty and complexity will become even more prevalent, which makes emotional intelligence an important skill for everyone to develop.

So, what is emotional intelligence? As we covered in the last chapter, it means understanding and expressing your emotions, and being empathetic when communicating with others. Although it may come more naturally to some, emotional intelligence is a set of skills that everyone can work on and develop. In this chapter we'll explore coaching strategies that have been designed to support you in your journey of developing, nurturing and enhancing your emotional intelligence.

◎ PERSONAL REFLECTION EXERCISE

One of the key aspects of emotional intelligence is being self-aware. Recognizing your emotions can help you to control how you react to difficult situations in your working environment. Although it isn't particularly useful to label emotions as 'good' or 'bad', because experiencing a wide range of emotions can be an important part of living a rich and meaningful life, there may be times that you would prefer not to be driven by intense emotions when reacting to challenging events while in a working environment.

Emotions such as passion and excitement can be valuable at work, but emotions don't always serve our best interests when it comes to interacting with others. For example, in situations where we perceive the stakes to be high – a tight deadline, a big meeting with the boss or an important client presentation – it can be easy to react out of fear or anxiety. Situations like these, moments of frustration with colleagues, or personal circumstances can act as triggers and lead to unfavourable responses.

Being aware of your triggers and resulting emotional reactions means you can be deliberate in how you respond to others and to events – which makes it more likely that you'll achieve something positive from the situation. By managing your emotions and behaviour, you can focus on finding solutions instead of dwelling on experiences, and you will feel more confident in tackling challenges. This doesn't mean you should suppress your emotions, or teach yourself not to feel them. Rather, it means learning from what your emotions are telling you and using that information to choose how to respond to situations.

Understanding how and why you have reacted to situations requires reflection and feedback, which can be facilitated in two ways – personal reflection, and feedback from others. Both ways of gathering information are important. Personal reflection provides an opportunity for you to pause and consider the emotions you feel in various situations at work, and how this impacts your behaviour. Feedback from others provides an insight into how you come across to others, who may not understand the emotional responses you experience, but they can provide a perspective on how your behaviour appears to others, and its impact on them. The reflection and feedback information combined will help to build your self-awareness.

There are questions you can ask yourself to build your understanding of how and why you react the way you do. You can use the template in Table 9.1 to help with this exercise. First up, take some time to consider either a specific event in the past, or a series of similar events – such as presenting (same task) to different stakeholders (executed in different ways). Start by describing the situation in as much detail as you can. This is where you want to note the context of the situation – include details such as the lead-up to the event, and why this was similar or dissimilar to other situations you've encountered before.

Next, think about the feelings you experienced. Be as honest and specific as you can be; remember this reflection tool is for you, and doesn't need to be shared with anyone. Imagine the context was presenting in front of senior stakeholders, which you've done before. But this time the stakes are even higher, you didn't have a huge amount of time to prepare, you don't have all the information you need, and you need to tackle a contentious issue whereby your team and a different team want to take completely different approaches to solve a problem.

You may be feeling anxious, overwhelmed, fearful or even excited. Note down as many feelings as you can. Next, note down how you reacted. Again, be honest here and don't apportion blame either to yourself or others, as that isn't the point of this exercise. Maybe you lacked confidence when presenting, and you didn't make the points you wanted to. Perhaps you feel like you may have come across as nervous, or defensive. Maybe you didn't handle questioning well after the presentation.

Finally, consider how you would approach the situation in the future. You may not be able to change the context or circumstances, and perhaps not even your feelings about the event. But you can learn to manage the feelings, first by identifying what's going on for you emotionally and using techniques such as breathing (which we'll cover later in this chapter) or separation, where you understand your feelings are valid and part of the process but they don't represent you as a person (Chapter 5 has exercises that can help with this approach). You may even consider that you could be honest with your stakeholders and mention it's a challenging topic, or you may not have all the information you need.

You might decide that you wouldn't change anything about the situation, but you would be kinder to yourself and manage your self-talk in a more productive way. So instead of beating yourself up about feeling that you're not getting something right or not achieving what is expected of you, remind yourself you're doing your best with the information you have and in the situation you find yourself in.

The template in Table 9.1 can be a useful way to frame the reflection process. It doesn't mean that you won't react

TABLE 9.1   Personal reflection template

Event description	
Feelings experienced	**How I reacted**
⚙	
⚙	
⚙	
How I would approach the same situation in the future	

to events in the future, but the process of reflection over time can help you to take a breath and pause before reacting to events, and you can then choose how to respond. Over time, this can help to build your confidence and stronger relationships with others.

◎ GATHERING FEEDBACK EXERCISE

Understanding how your behaviour and actions come across to others is the second part of building your self-awareness. We view events and interactions from one perspective, which is shaped by our experience and knowledge, but there are many ways most interactions could be interpreted. At times we all have personal blind spots making it difficult to assess our development areas and appreciate how our actions are perceived; gathering perspectives from others is one of the most effective ways to unveil these.

Broadening your perspective with feedback is both a science and an art, but how do you effectively ask for feedback? Keep in mind that people often find it hard to provide feedback as they're concerned that anything other than praise could be taken as a criticism (which may not be the way the feedback was intended to be delivered). My advice is to make the event of asking for feedback as informal and low-key as possible, so it makes the other person comfortable in sharing their thoughts. I would simply ask a variety of people you trust the same question: *What could I do even better?*

This creates a safe space for others to provide developmental feedback where they're pointing out something you could change. But the feedback also doesn't have to be delivered as a criticism. It could be that you're doing something well, and you could tweak your approach slightly to do that same thing exceptionally well.

Often it helps to provide some context when you're asking for feedback, so you could explain that presentations aren't going well for you, or you're not seeing the reaction you're expecting from others. Ask those you trust how they perceive the situation and what you could do to make the results even better, or what *they* would do in this situation to create even better results.

If you make the process easy for those providing feedback, so they feel comfortable and don't need to prepare too much, you're much more likely to receive helpful feedback. Once you've gathered feedback, you must choose how to use it. I have four tips:

1 **Take a step back**. When you receive feedback that you don't like or perhaps don't initially agree with, your ego can sometimes get in the way, which can cause you to react negatively. We can also take feedback in different ways depending on what mood we're in, so it's always a good idea to take some time to process it. Remember that we all have development areas and room to improve – it's what we do with that information that's important. Let the other person know that you've heard and understood their feedback and will take it on board. Assuming that it has been delivered in an appropriate way, someone has given you advice intended to help you, so always be gracious and grateful for the insight.

2 **Don't fixate on the negative** or **the positive**. Take a balanced view of any feedback you receive and look at it from all angles to gain a rounded perspective.

An overly positive view of yourself (where you don't take constructive feedback on board) is unrealistic and can cause blind spots, but the opposite, where you only fixate on developmental feedback and not positive feedback you may have received, can be deflating and demotivating. We're hardwired to focus more on negative feedback, so try to avoid doing this. While it's important to appreciate feedback and use it constructively, try not to fixate on it.

3 *Separate opinion and fact.* Always keep in mind that developmental feedback is only one person's point of view, and someone else might think completely differently. One opinion doesn't always provide an accurate picture, so focus on the facts and consider different perspectives. Ask a few people for the same feedback – this will help you see patterns and development themes.

4 *Create a forward focus.* Your thoughts and feelings create the story that you tell yourself, and the same applies when you're receiving feedback. Knowing how you can improve on past performance and behaviours is useful, but it's not something that you should dwell on or feel bad about. Instead, commit to creating your story moving forward. Considering all points of view, how can you use the information to grow and develop? Maybe you could come up with a plan to develop in areas where you're not performing as well, based on the feedback you've received.

When you're gathering feedback, make it a broad process whereby you ask for feedback from multiple perspectives. Ask people you trust for their advice and opinions, accumulate the information and look for key themes and creative ideas.

◉ BREATHING EXERCISE

Learning how to calm yourself with breathing techniques can enable you to take the heat out of challenging situations, slowing your response to challenges and providing you with more time to react in a way you *choose* to, rather than reacting automatically. This is part of the self-management process of building emotional intelligence.

As you may remember from the previous chapter, our responses to events that happen around us are incredibly quick. You may find yourself in a heated situation, and within a split second you've experienced an emotional response and have reacted with your actions or behaviour. Focusing on your breathing when you experience intense emotions has two benefits. Firstly, slowing your breathing can help to regulate intense emotions, softening the intensity of the feelings you're experiencing. Breathing impacts your heart rate, which can result in calming your body and mind. Secondly, the time you spend focusing on breathing breaks the link between experiencing emotions and responding immediately, providing you with some time to choose how you respond, ideally once the emotional intensity has reduced. There are two techniques you can use to regulate your breathing:

1 ***Focus on calming with exhaling***. Breathing out intensely, or for longer periods of time, reduces your heart rate, which has a calming effect, counteracting the effects of stress.[1] When you feel your emotions start to rise or your heart rate quicken, before focusing on anything else, take a few moments to focus on exhaling deeply, which will start to bring your heart rate down. Once

you've achieved this, you can then take a moment to choose how to respond to a challenging situation or person. This way, you're not reacting in the heat of the moment or automatically – you're giving yourself time to react in a considered way. This doesn't mean the emotions you experience should be ignored, or you want them to disappear, it just means you'll use the emotional experience to shape your response, not fuel it.

2 **Box breathing to pause**. Another breathing technique you may find useful is the idea of breathing in a box shape, as seen in Figure 9.1. The idea is you visualize a box as you breath in and out. So, breathe in for the count of four and imagine drawing the first side of a box, breath out for four and imagine drawing the second side. Then in again for the count of four and imagine drawing the third side of a box, and out again for four – the fourth side of the box. Repeat this for 30 seconds to a minute. The point of this exercise is to focus on something else other than the event or situation taking place and give yourself time before deciding how to respond. This approach means you're much more likely to respond in a considered and effective way.

◎ MAKE SENSE WITH YOUR SENSES EXERCISE

Social awareness – or the ability to understand how others are feeling and respond to their needs – is hugely important when it comes to creating strong and collaborative relationships. Social awareness is the process of building a picture of what is going on around you, which can include understanding others, interpreting situations and getting

FIGURE 9.1 Box breathing

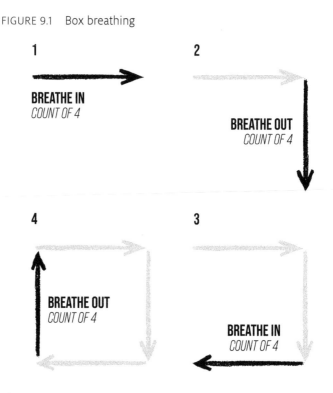

clear on the organizational culture you're operating within. Building social awareness is about picking up on cues around you and interpreting the information you gather to inform how you interact with others (the relationship management aspect of emotional intelligence).

Although some people find it easier than others to pick up on social cues, this is a skill that can be learned by focusing on your senses. The idea is you start to pay attention to what your senses are telling you about your surroundings. Focus on:

- what you can hear
- what you can see
- what you can smell
- what you can taste
- what you can feel

In a workplace setting, you're more than likely going to focus on the first two senses in this list – sound and sight. You can practise this skill in meetings. Take a moment to focus just on the facts – what you can see and hear – without using any judgement (this also doubles up as a mindfulness exercise).

This may be easier to do when you're in the same room as other people. Reading this information in a virtual environment through a screen can be tricky, but it is possible. You may need to focus a bit more to gather information. You may notice that a colleague looks disengaged, or they're not paying attention. You may hear some tension in someone's tone of voice. Often, you're picking up on these cues subconsciously; this exercise makes the process conscious, and trains your brain to pay attention to subtle clues that can help you to understand what's going on around you.

Once you've noticed these cues, think about what the information tells you. You don't necessarily want to create a story about the facts – for example, you won't know if tension in someone else's tone is aimed at you – but you might be able to piece this information together later to provide intuitional insight. For example, maybe your colleague's tone or body language changed when talking about a particular topic.

Working with social cues can be exhausting for some people, and if that's the case you might want to book in some rest where you can switch off between meetings or social events. You can also work on these skills outside of the workplace; you could conduct a 'sensory audit' where you purposely take time out to absorb and interpret information around you – perhaps by taking a walk outside in nature, or a stroll through the office to notice small details.

Once you start to notice and interpret social information, the next step is using that to consider how to interact with others to build strong relationships.

◎ INTENT AND IMPACT REFLECTION EXERCISE

How you *intend* to come across to others may not be how you *actually* come across. When considering how to communicate effectively with others, it can be easy to fixate on the message you want the other person to hear, and how best to construct and deliver that message. This is an important factor when developing your communication skills, but it's only part of the process when developing your relationship management skills. This is because relationships are built on more than communication, they're built on impact.

What exactly creates an impact with someone else, you may be wondering? Impact is the message received by the other person about you and what you're saying. There are a host of factors that influence how others perceive you, such as the words you use, tone, body language, empathy displayed, clarity of ideas, behaviours, values, trust. The truth is, it's very difficult to control exactly how you impact another person, because some of the impact will be shaped by the other person's perspective, values and expectations. Over time, however, you can work to create an impact over several interactions, which will be directed by building trust with others – being consistent in your words and actions, recognizing their needs and doing what you say you will.

Although impact is tricky to categorize, and you won't always know the exact impact you've had on others unless they tell you, you can work with clues. Think about a challenging encounter you've had with a colleague – what made that interaction so difficult? Take a moment to dissect what you know about the other person's perspective in this situation – what were they expecting from you? Why did they not respond positively? Where did the interaction start to go wrong?

This is an exercise you can repeat when you're experiencing a conflict at work, or challenges with others. The template in Table 9.2 may help you to execute this strategy. Before an interaction, focus on your intent. What is it you want to achieve in the meeting? Do you need to share knowledge? Gain approval? Achieve a specific outcome? Make the other person feel valued and included? Think to yourself, what do I want the other person to take away from this interaction?

Then consider how you'll make the impact you want to achieve – will you use empathy? Highlight how trustworthy you are? Build rapport? Be clear with the facts? Be honest? Open? Friendly? Firm? You'll want to match your tone, language and body language to help you communicate your intention.

After the meeting, it's important to take some time to reflect on the impact you made. You may receive this

TABLE 9.2   Intent and impact template

Pre-meeting preparation

What I want to achieve (intention)	How I plan to achieve it
⬤	⬤
⬤	⬤
⬤	⬤

Post-meeting reflection

Impact I made (based on explicit or implied feedack)	What I don't yet know about the situation
⬤	⬤
⬤	⬤
⬤	⬤

Gaps between intent and impact	Next steps
⬤	⬤
⬤	⬤
⬤	⬤

information explicitly, for example if the other person says, 'I just can't back this plan', or 'You've convinced me'. Often, however, you'll have to use other information that isn't explicit – things like tone or body language, feedback or opinions from others about the interaction, or maybe over time it'll become clear how the other person feels if they don't stick to the plans they agreed with you.

While you're reflecting, consider what you don't know about the situation. You might reflect that you have no idea whether the other person is championing your project, or thinks your plans are a worthwhile venture. You may not know whether they generally feel positive or ambivalent towards you. Things you don't know will be unique to every situation, and as the saying goes, sometimes you don't know what you don't know. This is totally acceptable; you're not expected to have all the answers here. This part of the exercise is about training yourself to at least *consider* whether there are any gaps in the information you have, which over time will help you to notice these knowledge gaps and start to narrow them.

The final reflection step is to identify gaps between your intent and impact. You may have intended to come across as supportive, but it seems, or becomes apparent, that the other person perceived you as a nuisance. Maybe you wanted to be decisive and finalize a strategy for your function for the following year, but your meeting was hijacked by another topic, so you weren't perceived as decisive at all (possibly because you didn't have the opportunity to be, or you didn't create the opportunity to be – in this example you could consider that in your reflection).

Finally, consider next steps. If you didn't come across how you wanted to, how do you change that in the future? *Can* you change that – do you have that control over the situation? It's important to set a plan about how to align your impact with your intent, but also be clear on where you can control the outcome of your interactions, and where you can't.

◎ INTERACTING WITH EMPATHY EXERCISE

The ability to empathize with people is a key component of emotional intelligence, and another critical factor in developing connections. When you empathize, you put yourself in someone else's shoes and look at a situation from their perspective. This helps to identify how the other person might feel, react and behave in different situations. This information can help you to understand and plan how to best communicate with individual people you work with.

Using emotional intelligence at work helps to promote constructive conflict, which is a critical element of a high-performing, productive and effective team. In a crisis, empathy becomes an even more crucial way to help build strong relationships. Empathy provides you with contextual information about the world the individual is operating within, which although you may not be able to relate to, you can appreciate. In the past, you may have experienced challenging situations with colleagues, and later realized that how that person reacted or behaved was influenced by stresses they were experiencing. Understanding this is a key factor in building collaboration and strong relationships across organizations.

Although some of us find empathy easier to demonstrate than others, there are three key steps everyone can learn to build empathy:

1 Ask the other person questions to find out more about what they're experiencing and how they feel about the situation and the impact it's having on them.
2 Consider the possibilities of how someone may think and feel. You don't necessarily have to know exactly what the other person feels, and you don't need to have had the exact same experience to imagine what the situation may be like for them. You just need to take what you know about that person and their circumstance and imagine how they would feel, react, behave and think about the situation.
3 Offer support and understanding by using phrases such as 'I imagine that *could* make you feel...' or 'I suppose that situation *could* make you think...'. It's best not to use definite statements such as 'It *must* make you feel...' or 'It *doesn't* seem...'. The reason for this is you want the other person to know you understand how they feel, but you need to acknowledge you don't know exactly what the situation is like for them. So, use tentative, exploratory language and words such as *could, possibly, maybe*.

Displaying empathy is a skill and requires a certain amount of balance. For example, you don't want to necessarily assume you know exactly what a situation is like for someone else, as that can be counterproductive, and rather than strengthening a relationship, this approach can be damaging. You could alienate the other person if your assumptions are incorrect. When considering how someone else may feel about a situation, it's important to remember you're not looking for the right answer, as only the other person knows exactly how they think and how they feel; rather, you're trying to imagine some of the possibilities. The only way you truly know how someone else feels is when they share that information with you.

Another tip when displaying your empathy is not to agree with everything the other person says, constantly finding examples that illustrate when you've faced the exact same challenges or situations. Although people generally behave like this with the best intentions, as they want the other person to know they understand the experience or challenge, it can be irritating for the other person if you always have an example that brings the conversation back to you. Again, the key here is balance. You can share your experiences to build rapport and demonstrate support, but also ask questions to find out more about how the other person feels and how they have interpreted the situation.

Overall, the benefit of empathizing is that you get a better insight into how someone else is thinking and feeling, and it gives you the opportunity to build stronger relationships. Ultimately, most people want to be understood, and they want to make connections with others, whether that be in their work or personal life. This principle is even more important in situations that are complex, stressful or uncertain, as this is often where relationships break down. If you can lead your communication and relationship management with empathy, even when you don't agree with the other person, you'll have a better shot at finding collaborative solutions and having open conversations. Ultimately, over time, this approach will create high-performing teams, made up of high-performing individuals.

The exercises in this chapter have been designed to be used as part of a long-term strategy to help you develop your emotional intelligence over time. You may find you want to use some of these tools immediately, and others you may want to come back to later. In the next chapter we'll delve into creating a coaching strategy that works for you, being smart about where you invest your energy when it comes to working on your mindset at work and being agile in your approach to professional and personal development to help you navigate the changing and complex world of work today, and in the future.

CHAPTER 10

Connection

When I set out to write this chapter, my intention was to write about purpose at work as a powerful tool to help navigate change and uncertainty. In fact, I wrote that chapter, but it wasn't great. The research was limited, case studies were bland, and it felt like one long unhelpful social media post full of buzzwords, written to incite radical change, while potentially making people feel unhappy about their lives in the process.

I knew I couldn't get behind the idea of purpose at work, even though I'm hearing from the Mindset Matters community that purpose is something we want at work. I mulled over this problem for some time – I had to write a chapter, but I also had to believe in what I was writing. I had to be willing to stand behind my words, put a stake in the ground and say this is an important topic to discuss if we want to navigate change effectively. And I just couldn't do that.

After some time and thought (mainly in the shower, while walking and in the gym – see Chapter 5 for notes on unconscious problem solving), I found some clarity on what the issue is for me. The idea of purpose is huge, and sometimes overwhelming or unobtainable. You may be lucky enough to know what your purpose in life is, and you may be even luckier to find that in your working life, but we don't all experience it. The idea of finding purpose can be scary, and honestly, I think at times elitist. Sometimes we must work to survive, to support ourselves, or as a stepping-stone for what we're trying to achieve – I've certainly been there. Even today, I've created the career I want, I've created a job that I never could have imagined existed. But am I working with purpose every day? No. I have an idea of what I'm working towards and it's hugely important that I help others on their career paths, but I can't hang my identity on a 'purpose', it's just too risky when things don't go to plan – I've been there, and you can feel broken when what you feel is your purpose is threatened.

I also don't assume that everyone wants the same things from work as me. My husband, for example, never has, and never will find purpose in his work. It may seem strange that I'm an occupational psychologist married to someone who doesn't identify themselves by their work, but he has another perspective about work, which may be different to mine, but it's just as valid (check out Chapter 4 where I talk about the power of alternative perspectives).

I also had a long journey to get to where I am today in my working life, and I will never forget or disregard the roles that helped me to pay for my education and experience.

If you'd asked me as a new graduate, completely overwhelmed and out of my depth, working in my first City job, what my purpose was, I would have frozen like a deer in headlights. No one ever asked me this (maybe the idea of purpose is a new phenomenon) but I imagine I would have thought it was about being financially secure (with a student loan hanging over my head) or having fun with my friends and colleagues on a Thursday and Friday night, or figuring out how to get a promotion as quickly as possible. I didn't necessarily have a purpose – and maybe you don't either. But I'm also not convinced we *need* purpose at work to be happy. Maybe it's a nice-to-have. I actually believe this the idea of finding your one true purpose at work can breed toxicity – consider the rise of information we're bombarded with on social media about how critical it is to work with purpose to be even remotely happy with our lives (coupled with the implication that no purpose is equal to a mediocre life). This kind of message is fuelled by the productivity hype we're seeing more and more of – with messages that explicitly state if you're not up working by 5 am, you're losing at life, which is a narrative I wholeheartedly disagree with.

A concept I do believe in, however, is meaning at work. You may think to yourself purpose, meaning, what's the difference? Actually, there's a clear distinction. Meaning is the emotional significance of actions you take and is shaped by the importance we ascribe to something. Things we value in life (our values) are part of what creates meaning for us, these are things that we need in order to feel satisfied and content. Meaning is a motivator – consider how often you do something because of the meaning it holds for you – going out of your way to help others, focusing on outcomes that positively affect others not just yourself, supporting or driving charitable endeavours. Purpose, on the other hand, is a much more complex construct – it's the aim of your life, the reasons you get up in the morning. Purpose is a huge deal. It can guide decisions, shape the goals you set for yourself and influence the actions you take day to day. Your purpose is your life's direction. Meaning, on the other hand, can consist of small moments that make your day feel worthwhile.

When I got to the crux of it, what I really believed that we needed to thrive in the workplace of today and the future was *connection*. Connection with others, connection to a sense of meaning and connection to community. So, I pivoted (check out Chapter 5, which delves into how agility is essential in the workplace today), and I'll explore each of these areas of connection in this chapter. In the next chapter I'll outline ways you can build connection into your working life.

Connecting with others

Workplaces that prioritize connecting people with one another to form strong bonds and networks are often the organizations that report higher employee motivation and engagement. In 2019, the organization Great Place to Work found that 89 per cent of those that featured in the

Fortune 100 best places to work were reported as being a workplace where you can count on people to cooperate, compared with 74 per cent of employees in other organizations.[1] Forming bonds with colleagues creates connection – which results in teams feeling more comfortable seeking help, providing feedback and taking part in open discussions. Over time, this can play a role in boosting innovation, motivation and psychological safety, which are all critical elements in a healthy organizational culture.

In today's workplace we're witnessing the rise of remote or flexible working, increased shift work to meet flexible customer needs, and people employed to work on parts of projects based on skills, or to reach a specific outcome rather than being expected to work the traditional 9-to-5. In short, the working world is more flexible and fluid than ever before. These new working norms create many benefits – less commuting, more time to spend with people you care about, fitting work around other commitments, a more satisfying work–life blend, to name a few. But when it comes to boosting satisfaction at work, there is one critical element that could suffer in the new set-up – building connection with others.

Connection at work has always been the cornerstone of creating strong relationships and developing powerful networks, which over time help to support career progression. Whether it's developing a relationship with a potential career sponsor who will be championing you in discussions about new opportunities that may be coming up, or colleagues showcasing your work and achievements when project teams are being configured, relationships matter. There's an argument to suggest relationships are just as important as skills and experience when it comes to career development.

Not only do strong relationships play a role in career development, but as UCLA professor Matthew Lieberman explains in his book *Social*, our need to connect socially is fundamentally a basic human need like shelter, food and water.[2] This in part may explain why we're so interested in the stories of others, whether that be in a television format by watching reality television or soap operas, or on social media where we're keen to learn more about the experiences of others. Lieberman states that social interactions can have such an impact on our lives that students have been found to remember information learned in social settings more accurately than when learning alone, and studies have shown that feeling liked and respected at work can be as rewarding and motivating as financial compensation. Whichever way we look at it, connection at work is crucial to promoting wellbeing and productivity, and to supporting career development.

Connecting teams

Building a culture of connection in part relies on the actions of leaders within the organization. At management software company Bento for Business, the focus on the power of relationships is a core component of supporting professional and personal development.[3] Senior leaders across the business are encouraged to share stories and experiences, and to offer mentorship to discuss challenges and goals, both inside and outside of work. The company encourages people to feel comfortable collaborating with senior leaders, or garnering advice from senior colleagues. One-to-ones with colleagues across roles and teams, regardless of seniority, are an approach that fosters a supportive and mentor-led culture. Their business motto is 'Be Human', a slogan chosen as a reminder of the fact people and relationships are the cornerstones of innovation and building great technology. This extends to helping one another as people and not just as co-workers, and this approach applies to colleagues, customers and partners.

The HR technology company Workday leads the way when it comes to championing connected teams. The executive team at Workday value making connections in the workplace and believe building strong social networks helps employees collaborate more effectively, share information well and support each other's growth and development, leading to greater individual satisfaction and motivation. They have embedded this idea into their company culture and offer all new hires a chance to take part in their New Connections programme – a full-day event that explores the importance of building strong relationships and helps employees make new connections both internally and externally, as well as strengthening existing ones.[4] Oliver McKenna, a Chief Technology Officer at Workday, emphasizes the role of connection at work. He believes that if people are inspired, engaged and, most importantly, connected at work, the customer experience is improved. In an increasingly flexible and fluid working environment, this is particularly important.[5]

Marc Benioff, CEO of Salesforce, has strived to build the business around the Hawaiian concept of *Ohana* – the idea that families, whether by blood or chosen, are bound together and responsible for each other.[6] Strong connections are key to creating such a close-knit, collaborative ecosystem, which includes employees, customers and communities, and is a big part of Salesforce's culture. One example of this is the company's internal discussion group 'Who should I talk to?' Here, employees can ask questions or find the right person to bring something to, making it easier to connect those who would benefit from speaking to each other. For example, someone could get information on which development team to speak to about a new product idea or where best to direct certain feedback. This focus on connection helps to build strong relationships amongst colleagues, but also reinforces a connection to the business, reminding people that they're part of a connected and supportive network at Salesforce.

A collective mission is a powerful tool than can help teams to connect in order to navigate uncertainty

Successful teams are made up of individuals who are all working toward the same mission, and this becomes even more important for teams who don't work from the same physical space. When team members understand and are aligned with the goals, purpose and values of an organization, they are more motivated to contribute to them, and they are more likely to act and make decisions in accordance with these factors. A collective mission is a powerful tool that can help teams to connect in order to navigate uncertainty, deal with challenges and turn change into a positive experience – an opportunity to thrive.

Meaningful connection

Connection with others is essential in a productive, engaged and motivated workplace. But connection with others is only part of the story – we also need connection to our work. Today, many of us are seeking meaning in our work lives, which can be as simple as doing one thing a day that matters to you, or a grander process of working towards a greater purpose.

In 2019 almost two hundred leaders from companies such as Apple, Cisco, Johnson & Johnson, PayPal and Pepsi signed a purpose statement detailing commitments to creating an organizational culture that 'allows each person to succeed through hard work and creativity and to lead a life of meaning and dignity'.[7] This focus on providing the opportunity to make work meaningful is a direct response to the shifting world of work, whereby employees expect to find meaning in their work, customer loyalty is underpinned by ethical and social considerations and shareholders are increasingly aware that future profit will be directly correlated in part with fair, equitable and socially responsible company policies. Many people have worked in roles that have provided this for decades: consider those in vocational roles such as teachers, health care professionals or scientists – meaningful work isn't a new concept. According to the World Economic Forum, what is new, however, is a shift towards a desire for meaning in traditionally corporate roles, whereby the outdated goal of creating profit alone has been somewhat redesigned to incorporate profit *with* meaning.[8]

Living with meaning may be linked to living longer. In fact, researchers found that of 7,000 people that were interviewed, those that didn't have a strong sense of meaning in life were almost twice as likely to die prematurely that those who were clear on what was meaningful for them. Those who were clear on meaning were happier, more fulfilled and less likely to experience health concerns such as strokes and heart attacks.[9] This data also held true across demographics such as gender, race and income.

Meaning can feel like your North Star – something you're moving towards that's important to you. Incorporating meaning into your working life can act as a buoy, keeping you afloat when challenges become overwhelming. When work becomes complex, unpredictable and uncertain, connecting to the meaning behind your work can switch your perspective from focusing in on all the elements of the situation you can't control, towards considering what you can control to achieve something that holds importance for you. In this sense, being conscious of what provides meaning for you at work serves as a strategy in your toolkit to navigate challenges at work, while also promoting positive mental health as you build resilience, which can also positively impact your physical health.

This move towards wanting to find meaning at work may have been accelerated in recent years, but it was already becoming a priority at work a decade ago. *Harvard Business Review* was reporting on the phenomenon of employees stating that meaning is as important as salary way back in 2011.[10] Fast-forward to 2018, and *Harvard Business Review* is still reporting on the same issue, finding that 9 out of 10 people are willing to earn less money to do more meaningful work.[11] And then in 2019 most of the working population experienced a seismic shift in their working lives as working through the Covid-19 pandemic highlighted the need for connection and meaning at work. Although extreme lockdowns are largely over and we're starting to witness the pandemic move into an epidemic phase, the desire, even need, to find purpose at work has become more important than ever. Working through a pandemic has accelerated a trend that was already present in the workplace, and it's almost as if we can't unlearn the lessons we were forced to learn as the world changed so rapidly – we'll carry those lessons into the workplace of the future.

Authentic meaning

Meaning is personal and represents an avenue by which employees find fulfilment – it can't be manufactured. As an organization and leader, communicating, supporting and nurturing meaning can be a powerful way to build connection throughout a business, but it's essential that the reason this is a focus is to create a healthy workplace environment, whereby employees feel they can be themselves and work towards outcomes that are important to them, and customers feel they can connect to the positive outcomes the organization has set out to achieve. When considering your own meaning, it needs to feel important and significant to you, which is something we'll explore in the next coaching chapter.

Royal Dutch State Mines (DSM) is an organization that describes itself as a purpose-led science company and is a business that encourages employees to nurture their own authentic meaning. Right at the top of the corporate website, DSM proudly state the business purpose is to create brighter lives for all, so much so that people within the organization have redesigned the brand name DSM internally to stand for Doing Something Meaningful.[12]

DSM embeds purpose into its way of working and believes that this directly leads to better performance.[13] Leaders within the company encourage employees to focus on Doing Something Meaningful, every day. As a benefit of this ethos co-CEOs Dimitri de Vreeze and Geraldine Matchett are creating a culture where employees feel inspired to do their best work, thus also authentically driving success for the business. Matchett and de Vreeze believe that employees who have a truly customer-first mindset and care about what the company is delivering will be inspired to innovate authentically. Executives understand that an organization that embraces diversity and encourages team members to share and explore different perspectives is more likely to be collaborative. Those working in this collaborative environment are more likely to feel connected to their teams, their work and the organization.

The key to the DSM approach is encouraging *authentic* meaning. The organization has a mission and purpose, but it's crucial that employees find their own way to connect to that to do something meaningful. DSM focuses on markets such as dietary supplements, early life nutrition and sustainable automotive engineering. Employees at DSM may find their personal values align with a sustainable, ethical and healthy approach that the company take to creating products, but they may have their own sense of meaning. Maybe they're passionate about child health or creating food products that are good for the planet. Perhaps reducing carbon footprint and helping others to do this is important to others. You can replicate this in your own work life – where can you find meaning that aligns with your work?

Take other organizations that aren't always so explicitly meaning-led. In a coaching programme I ran with a multi-national banking organization, I was fascinated to observe how teams that recoup debt from customers talked about why their work holds so much meaning for them. Gone are the days of debt collection being a hard transaction. Rather, these teams were focusing on how they could genuinely assist the customer who may have fallen on hard times and help them to get back on their feet and manage the debt situation compassionately. From an outside perspective it could be easy to assume this would be an undesirable job – tense conversations, customers hanging up the phone or being abusive. And this can happen, but the people that excelled in these teams saw their job as one that helps, serves and supports those they're having these challenging conversations with. They display empathy and compassion, and above all they describe a sense of meaning.

Not everyone finds meaning in every part of their role, but it is possible to find a small amount of meaning in your working situation. If you consider some of the activities you take part in as part of your job, you might find there are elements that help others; perhaps the work you do benefits customers, clients or team members, and for you that feels important. Maybe meaning for you is about doing a good job and being proud of what you're achieving. Perhaps it's additional activities you take part in that make the difference for you – such as leading a committee or arranging charity events.

If you can frame your work around meaning, you're a lot more likely to be motivated, satisfied and interested at work. The key is to understand what holds meaning for you, and what you value in life, and weave that into your working life where you can. We'll explore ways to do this in the next coaching chapter.

What do you value?

As we explored in Chapter 4, connecting to your values at work can act as a stable anchor that keeps you focused on what's important to you, and connects you to why the work you do is important when you face challenging experiences. Focusing on the bigger picture, connecting to meaning and providing value for others are practices that can drive you forward when the reality feels tough. Often when I ask coaching clients where the meaning is for them at work, it can be a difficult question to answer – meaning isn't always explicit and often it's not specific actions or tasks that create meaning.

Take my work, for example. Meaning for me means helping people to feel able to navigate uncertainty and challenges successfully. When I'm replying to emails or trying to arrange podcast guests, I can't say I find the work meaningful. In fact, I often find it challenging – the process of contacting potential guests and generating interest can be tricky. But these actions are necessary for me to be able to work with meaning in general. If I want to genuinely help others navigate challenges, I need to provide the opportunity to hear from experts who have an opinion on this. I must look past the actions that may not be comfortable for me; in fact, I take myself out of the equation altogether. The process isn't about me and how I feel, it's about being committed to providing information that I know will help others. If you were to ask me day-to-day does my work provide meaning for me, I might struggle to find ways in which this is the case, as would people in many professions, I'm sure. Healthcare professionals, for example, may find parts of their roles challenging rather than meaningful. If you're struggling to identify meaning at work, start with understanding what you value in life, because your values are directly aligned with meaning. This is something we'll explore in the next coaching chapter.

Micro-meaning moments

At times, the broader picture of meaning at work may be clear – take my example of helping people to thrive in uncertainty. This may be enough to keep you moving forward when you hit roadblocks, or obstacles threaten to throw you off-course, but at times this bigger picture may not motivate you to keep moving forward with purpose. When you're feeling disconnected from your work, take some time to focus on what you *really* value in life, and consider where the micro-meaning moments at work are for you. Maybe it's taking extra time to help colleagues or customers in a small way. Perhaps it's providing support for a community at work that would benefit from your help. Maybe it's about focusing on your personal development or helping others to learn.

Reflecting on micro-meaning moments can be an effective tool to help gain clarity about what truly matters to you, which is, at the heart of it, about working in the service of something that is bigger than yourself. Whereas finding purpose or living with purpose can be a daunting prospect for some, finding the opportunity for small moments of meaning, and celebrating these activities, will help you to feel connected and engaged with your work, and over time can impact your motivation. Meaning doesn't have to be about a higher purpose; it's about connecting with your values and things in life that matter to you, and taking small steps in those areas. You may have no clue what your purpose in life is, and I don't necessarily consider this a bad thing at all – I'm not convinced we need to have purpose at work to be happy and satisfied. I do, however, believe that our work needs to mean something to us if we want to effectively navigate uncertainty, build resilience to adversity and stay motivated in an unpredictable environment. Meaning provides a reason to keep moving forward, find solutions and overcome challenges. You may be lucky enough to find your working life

Meaning provides a reason to keep moving forward, find solutions and overcome challenges.

meaningful in every way, but if this isn't the case for you, take a moment to consider where you do find meaning – it could be helping customers, dealing with issues to make life easier for clients, providing support for your colleagues. In the next coaching chapter, we'll delve into how to create and nurture micro-meaning moments.

Connection, meaning and community at work

Connection, in part, is about community. When you feel connected to other people, and connected to a sense of meaning, the next logical step is to nurture a sense of community. When you're part of a community, you find similarities with others, whereby you value the same things, you find meaning in similar places and you feel that you belong. Communities help us to feel that we're on a journey with other people, who may face similar challenges or experiences. They offer support, safety, and security. You may have experienced a time where you've felt part of a tribe – this is community at its finest.

We're all experiencing the effects of a complex, uncertain and changeable working life. Whether that be due to technological advancement, economic, political or social developments, or navigating the after-effects of a global crisis. You have a choice when it comes to how you approach your working life. You can be passive, where you feel that you can't change your circumstances or change course. Or you can take control and commit to taking small steps towards the future you want to create.

Coming together with others on the same personal and professional development journey will help you to tackle the challenges and complexities we all face in the workplace today and in the future. The Mindset Matters community has been built for exactly this reason, as a place to learn, connect and share with others who are focused on finding ways to not only survive in an uncertain world, but to thrive.

As connection becomes something we truly need at work, consider the communities you're part of, and those you're building. These collective spaces – whether that be physical or virtual – filled with people on the same path as you, who share your values and find meaning in similar ways could be the support system you need to navigate challenges and master a complex and uncertain working environment.

Collective support and meaning will be a key component of a successful career in the workplace of the future. In the next coaching chapter, we'll explore strategies and tools you can use to build connection with others, connection to meaning, and connection to a community in your work life.

CHAPTER 11

Coaching:
The meaning of connection

As we explored in the previous chapter, connection at work is no longer a nice-to-have, it's become an essential ingredient in navigating uncertainty and overcoming challenges – which, let's be honest, will affect all of us at one time or another. When you're facing tough times in your career, connection with others, connection with work that means something and a community you can rely on all have the potential to pull you through.

In a complex working world that is forever changing, we can't underestimate the power of connection. When the world around you feels unstable or overwhelming, connecting to someone, something or a group can be the support and grounding you need to help you take the next step.

This coaching chapter isn't a blueprint for building your network or building your social media connections. Although those approaches are practical and incredibly useful in your career, they don't address your mindset – how you think about connection – and mindset is what this book is about. You may find you want to focus on one aspect of connection, and maybe other areas later (or not at all). Follow your instinct, dive into what you're drawn to and test out the exercises to find out what works for you.

◎ CONNECTION MAPPING EXERCISE

Establishing both professional and personal networks that can offer guidance and encouragement will help you to navigate challenging and difficult situations. This also has the benefit of potentially boosting your resilience, helping you to overcome adversity and building your psychological strength to tackle obstacles in the future. There are various strands of a strong support system. Before starting the mapping exercise, consider the people you have genuine connections with. Here are some ideas to get you thinking:

- **Colleagues.** Building genuine connections with people in your workplace can ensure you create fulfilling, long-lasting relationships and in turn work better as a team, especially during stressful times. There are many ways to nurture workplace relationships, but it's particularly important to communicate when you need support and offer the same in return, take an active interest in co-workers' individual circumstances – both personally and within their role – and show that you're someone who can listen and build strong connections.

- **A mentor or coach.** Having someone you can count on for support or turn to for advice is helpful when navigating uncertainty at work. This could be a direct manager, someone within your organization who you trust and admire or a person in your field whose experiences and knowledge are relevant to your future goals. Building connections with people who can offer guidance can prove to be critical when it comes to deciding what steps to take next in your career, or when working through a complex situation. There are also benefits to being a mentor for others and building a connection that way, which can also be an activity that is meaningful for you.

- **Like-minded professionals.** Connecting with other people in your industry that understand your work can be a great way to expand your connections with others. There are plenty of online communities on social media platforms such as Facebook and LinkedIn, apps designed for networking, and industry-specific events to help you meet people who you can foster professional relationships with. At the heart of connecting with others is a feeling of being heard and understood. Building relationships with others who share similar interests can provide this in a meaningful way. This process is not only something that can help you to grow your support network, but it also has the added benefit that you're building a network of people who may be able to help you make positive career moves in the future.

- **Family and friends.** It's also important to have a support network outside the professional realm. In order to stay resilient when facing adversity, we need to have the energy to face the daily challenges we're presented with at work. Aside from lending a listening ear when we need one, our family and friends are key to a healthy work–life blend. All of us need time to relax, unwind and re-energize so that we can thrive at work. Consider the things that are most important for your emotional wellbeing and how you can incorporate them into your working week – whether it's quality time with your family, socializing, time for hobbies, exercise and mental stimulation, or a focus on recharging your energy with others.

To start this exercise, you can use the template in Figure 11.1 to map out the top 10 people you feel connected to right now (this may change over time). In each circle, write the person's name, and why you feel connected to that person (this could include observations such as they offer great advice, always listen, go out of their way to check in on me, offer light relief, know when I'm feeling down, etc). It may take some time to consider the people you're most connected to, which is completely fine – you may have never considered this before.

Finally, in the middle of the diagram, jot down notes about this group of people. You might want to note similarities, differences or themes. This will provide you with clues about the kind of people you connect well with if you're looking to expand your genuine connection circle. It may also highlight gaps whereby there are other kinds of people you'd like to build connections with (we tackle how to do this in the next exercise).

Consider how this map makes you feel. Does it change the way you view those you feel connected to? Or make you more focused on building more genuine connections in your life?

An optional part of the exercise is to let your connections know you appreciate them, and why. If you reflect on how positive you feel about the support you receive from those you connect with well, your appreciation may offer the same feeling for them.

FIGURE 11.1   Connection mapping template

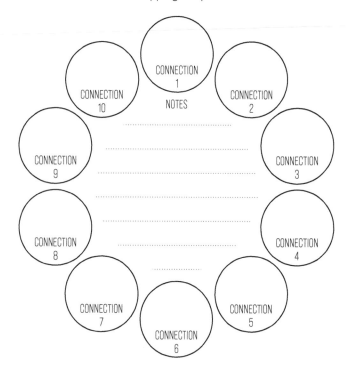

◎ BUILDING CONNECTED RELATIONSHIPS EXERCISE

The previous exercise may have highlighted where you have strong connections with others in your life – you may find you have these in the workplace or in other parts of your life. You may have filled all ten spots with names, or you may feel that you'd like to build more connections with others. As time goes on, the chances are you'll build connections with more people, which for some may be an easy process, and for others may be trickier at times. It can be useful to break down some of the steps that can help to build a strong connection with others, which can provide some pointers if this is a process you find challenging. Here are some areas to focus on:

- BUILDING TRUST

  This is where the other person believes in your character and integrity. Trust takes time to build; it's unlikely you'll build real trust with a few interactions. You can focus on building trust with others by consistently delivering on what you say you will, matching your words with your actions, and waiting for opportunities where you can demonstrate you are trustworthy. Although it can be tempting to fast-track trust building to create a strong relationship, this approach can be counter-intuitive as you may come across as being over-familiar. If you attempt to overly demonstrate your trustworthiness too soon, it can seem forced and disingenuous to the other person. In truth, you often need to play the long game when building trust, remaining focused on slowly and consistently building a relationship. To help build trust, you could use some of these techniques:

- Ask questions and take an interest in the other person.

- Share some information about yourself (about your professional or personal life).

- Be consistent in following up, and showing up in a way that makes the other person know you stick to your word.

- Be honest with your opinions, but also be kind – you can say what you need to say in the kindest possible way.

- Find ways to show you care.

- BEING AUTHENTIC

It can at times be tempting to mould yourself to the other person when you're trying to build a relationship, and in some ways this is a good idea. Consider Chapters 8 and 9, where I discuss using emotional intelligence to strengthen relationships. Part of this is being socially aware and adaptable in how you communicate with different people – often shaping your communication to the individual. It's important to be adaptable in how you interact, but it is just as important to be authentic. You shouldn't change who you are – this can make others feel uneasy, which can erode trust. When building trust, it pays to be authentically adaptable, being true to who you are, but deciding which parts of your personality or communication style you use. For example, you may have some friends or colleagues who appreciate quieter and deeper conversations, which you enjoy at times. You may interact with other people who are louder and prefer a crowd, which you also enjoy at times. You can connect with both kinds of people. Here are some ways you could focus on being authentic:

o   Make decisions and communicate in ways that align with your values (we'll cover that in the next exercise) and your beliefs.

o   When you feel comfortable to do so, allow yourself to be vulnerable with the other person at times.

o   Admit when you're wrong – we all must do this at times, and it's better for a relationship to admit when we made a mistake rather than covering it up or avoiding the situation.

o   Share your opinions and experiences – it's hard for people to connect with you if they don't know anything about you.

•   STRATEGIC CONNECTING
Being strategic may seem like a strange way to approach building genuine connections. You might be thinking that relationships just build naturally. The truth is, however, that building strong relationships takes time and commitment, and if you're not focused with a plan to consistently check in with others, the power of your connection can diminish. Here are some ways you can be strategic, as well as authentic, when building relationships:

o   Schedule time to focus on relationships – this could include putting reminders in your diary to check in with someone or keeping an hour free a week to contact people who you haven't heard from in a while.

o   Consider who you need to connect with this week. You might specifically need a friendly ear, some advice or a laugh. If you feel the need to connect with someone, make sure you check in, even if it's a quick message. Remember, we're talking about nurturing genuine connections here, not growing a professional network.

○ Reply promptly if someone you have a strong relationship with gets in touch. I know this isn't always easy, and we're all busy, but being consistent in responding is one way to build trust. You don't always have to get into a lengthy exchange, but you can choose to respond. If you miss this opportunity now and again it's not a big deal, but over time if you only engage at a time that works for you, the connection may weaken.

○ Be open to connecting with others. Your connection mapping template (Figure 11.1) may be full, but you still may come across interesting people you'd like to build a relationship with. Connection strength also changes over time, so some of your previous connections may become less intense, which may leave some room for you to develop new connections.

Consider how you make and nurture the genuine connections with others currently. Ask yourself:

- *How do you make and nurture connections well?*
- *How can you do this even better?*

◎ VALUE IDENTIFIER EXERCISE

Whether you're conscious of it or not, your values show up in all areas of your life. Your values are a deep-rooted, core part of who you are and how you think. They affect how you respond to events and the important decisions you make. Think of your values as principles and standards of behaviour. They're your judgement about what's important in life. Often, if you can identify your values, you'll find clues about what it is that creates meaning for you.

If I were to ask you right now what your core values are, would you be able to answer? Sometimes your values are crystal clear, and sometimes they're not so obvious. We don't always take the time to consider our personal values, and if we do, we don't always think about aligning those with our work.

Your values are fairly stable over time – they don't change a great deal from early adulthood. You may find your values change as your circumstances alter, such as becoming a parent may make you more family-oriented, which can change the way you view your career. It tends to be big events that change your values – if at all – and this happens slowly over time. As your values don't change overnight, it's essential to work in a way that fits with your personal values and outlook because, if you don't, that grating sense of something not being right at work will only magnify over time.

If you can find ways to work that align with your values, you'll most likely find parts of your work that you feel strongly connected to, that are meaningful for you. When navigating change and uncertainty, values and in particular a sense of meaning, provide a reason for you to find the motivation to keep moving forward and create solutions in tricky situations.

Here are some ways you can identify your values:

1 Make a list of the things you value in life. Don't consider how these translate into cut and dried values right now,

just jot down all the words that spring to mind when you think about what you value.

2 Use some prompts to add to your list. Consider times you felt proud about something you or others have done. Pride can often highlight something we value. Also think about people you admire – what is it about them you admire? And does this tell you anything about your values? Also consider when you feel at your best – what's going on in your life when that happens? Does this tell you anything about things you value in life?

3 Use a value list. You can download a version I use at my website (see page 1). You can either use the checkbox on your screen or print the list off and use a good old-fashioned pen-and-paper approach to tick the words that mean something to you. The chances are, quite a few words will stand out for you, as they're all positive words. You can go wild and tick as many as you like.

The next step is to whittle down your top values, which will be your guiding lights when it comes to connecting to your work (you can use the template in Table 11.1 to help with this). From the list(s) you've created, identify your top 10 values, the words you absolutely must keep (this may not be an easy exercise, it's hard to give up some of the positive words). It doesn't mean the words that don't make your top 10 list aren't relevant, they can still be values, but they may not be your strongest values.

Next up, consider your 'super-values' – these are your top five, which you'll need to whittle down from your top 10 list. Again, it doesn't mean those that don't make the list aren't important, rather we're trying to identify what's *really* important to you. Next consider what your anti-values might be – these are the absolute opposite of your values, and things that are likely to destroy your connection with work. For example, you could have this split:

SUPER VALUES	ANTI-VALUES
Fun	Seriousness
Gratitude	Ungratefulness
Achievement	Lack of recognition
Fairness	Unfairness
Collaboration	Selfishness

Your anti-values may not be exact opposites of your super values, which is totally fine. If you experience anti-values in your working life, the chances are a sense of meaning will be severed.

Finally, consider where you use your values at work – these could be the parts of your work that create meaning for you. You might also want to consider if and how you could create more meaning in your working life by reducing your exposure to anti-values, which might feel toxic to you, and increase your use of super-values.

When you've completed this exercise, take some time to ponder how it makes you feel. Would you consider yourself connected to some of your work? Would you like to increase this or replicate it in other areas of your life? If you want to build connection and meaning in your work, it's important to do something with this information you've discovered through reflection and use it to guide the choices you make about next steps. Does this exercise make you think any differently about your work?

TABLE 11.1   Value mapper template

Top 10 values

1	6
2	7
3	8
4	9
5	10

Super values	**Anti-values**
1	1
2	2
3	3
4	4
5	5

Where I use my values in my working life	**How I could find more meaning at work**
●	●
●	●
●	●
●	●

◉ MICRO-MEANING MOMENT EXERCISE

If your work holds meaning for you, you're more likely to be motivated, feel satisfied with your working life and be empowered to find solutions when faced with challenges. It can be tricky to know where to start when creating a sense of meaning; it can feel like a huge, overwhelming task at times. If, however, you focus on small moments of meaning, you can harness the benefits of meaning in your working life without experiencing a sense of pressure or being overwhelmed by the thought of identifying your purpose.

If you can learn to focus on the small moments that create meaning for you, your sense of connection with your work can be strengthened, and you can commit to creating more of these meaning moments in your working day.

You can use the template in Table 11.2 as a guide to support you in reflecting on the moments that create meaning for you. It can be useful to acknowledge these moments regularly, perhaps at the end of every day. Ideally you want this to be a quick and simple exercise; the less cumbersome the reflection, the more likely you are to take part in it. You might also want to practise this at the same time as you practise other habits (such as brushing your teeth or shutting off your computer at the end of the day), so you start to associate the two activities and your reflection becomes built into your routine.

The first step is to consider small moments that meant something to you in your working life today. These can be simple activities such as supporting a network of individuals who need your help, going above and beyond for

TABLE 11.2   Micro-meaning reflection template

Plan to build more micro-meaning moments into my life over the coming week	Micro-meaning moments experienced today
1	1
2	2
3	3

Reflection: meaning themes

-
-
-

vulnerable customers, championing projects that are important to you at work, a chat with someone you care about, supporting a colleague, being on the receiving end of gratitude, creating something important to you. You can then use this information to plan how to build more meaning into your working life over the coming week. Of course, some meaning will be unexpected, such as a kind message from someone else. But you may be able to create some meaning in other ways. For example, imagine a moment of meaning was a creative activity you took part in – there could perhaps be ways you can do more of this over the next week.

Finally, reflect on themes that are emerging for you. Are there specific activities that create meaning for you? Are there particular people that create meaning for you? Or in fact, is the opposite the case – are there people that drain meaning from your working life? Or activities that threaten your sense of meaning? You can use this information to shape your working life in the future to create and celebrate more micro-meaning moments.

◎ SETTING VALUES-BASED GOALS EXERCISE
Working with values-based goals will help you to make decisions to move towards work that matters to you, and encourage you to be more flexible as things change. Values tend to stay relatively stable over time, but they can shift – usually depending on where we are in life. For example, earlier in your career, you may place more importance on progression, whereas when you're more established in your career, you may also value time to pursue interests outside of work. If you have a goal that no longer serves you, you may need to find the courage to change course. Trying things and getting different types of experience are important but so is being honest with yourself when it's time to explore other possibilities. If you're pursuing your values and seeing goals as part of the journey instead of the destination, when you're forced to change your direction you'll view this as a pivot and a twist in the road rather than a failure.

When it comes to goal setting, it's important to work with your values, which is a topic I discussed in detail with Richard MacKinnon in a Mindset Matters live interview.[1] You may have experienced the effects of toxic goal setting, whereby you're so focused on the target you're trying to achieve, that you forget to check in to determine whether this end-goal, and how you're trying to achieve it, fits with what matters to you in life. Often, when you finally reach these goals, they can feel empty, or you may find that you've caused some damage to your health or relationships along the way.

If you don't have a values-based direction, you can very easily get caught up in other people's goals, or goals that you think you *should* have, but actually aren't important to you at all. Even if you attain these, it can often feel empty. Not having a sense of meaning can also lead to becoming too goal-oriented in an unsustainable way. For example, you'll think that finally getting a promotion will make you happy, but when you do, it becomes the 'new normal' and you need to set a different, more challenging goal.

When you have clarity on what matters to you, you can use your values as tools that help you achieve meaningful goals, rather than being blinded by arbitrary goals that may be important to others, but not necessarily you.

Here are some ways you can start to focus on values-based goals:

1 **Get clear on your values** (the previous exercise can help with this) but acknowledge that your values may change over time. So, regularly check and reflect on whether your values have changed or shifted position (you may

find one of your top-five values moves further down the list and another moves into one of your top-five 'super values' spots.

2 **Set yourself meaningful goals.** Rather than aiming for a promotion, a particular salary or a specific position, make the goal something that holds meaning for you, that you connect to. You may find that a goal of being promoted actually *is* meaningful for you because it will mean you're more financially secure, which creates security for your family, or you'll be doing work that is important to you. Connect to this meaning and make that your goal – so, in this case, security for your family or meaningful work. The beauty of this approach is it means you don't have to get that specific promotion, as there may be other ways to achieve security or meaning at work.

3 As Richard MacKinnon suggests in the Mindset Matters interview, **cultivate habits around your goals.** If you set yourself a goal of more focus on family and less on work at the weekends, you could make it a habit to generally not check emails at the weekend. Alternatively, if your goal is to work towards a qualification to create more security and meaning in your work, consider what habits could facilitate this. In this case, you might want to generally study at weekends, or build a habit where you study before you start work.

4 With values-based goals, the aim is to **lose the binary expectations,** such as 'I will *never* work on weekends' or 'I study *every* day'. Some days or weekends you just won't facilitate this. Life isn't static; demands will increase at times and wane at others. If you have very

fixed goals, when you can't meet these goals (such as when you have an important presentation on Monday morning and you need to run through your presentation on Sunday to feel confident, breaking your 'rule' of no weekend working), you're going to feel that you've failed. Therefore, Richard MacKinnon suggests focusing on principles rather than rules. This gives you flexibility in applying your values – a principle of family time, for example, could take a different form every week.

5 Finally, **don't compare yourself to others** or set goals with anyone other than yourself in mind. Instead, check in with where you are today versus where you were yesterday or last year. Ask yourself if you're happy with the decisions and the progress that you've made, and if not think about what you can do differently going forward. Have regular reviews with yourself and think about what you've learned and how you can be mindfully aware of where you're going.

Goals are only useful if we know why we're setting them, how they're relevant to us, and how they fulfil the kind of person we want to be. Set yourself the challenge of relying less on binary goals and focus more on values-based goals.

◎ BUILDING COMMUNITY EXERCISE

Being part of a community at work is so important in today's business environment. Many of us are almost craving connection with others and a sense of belonging that comes with being part of a supportive community, made up of people on a similar journey, or those with similar interests. There are so many ways to connect with a community. Consider online groups, meet-up events (in real life and virtual), volunteer groups, co-working communities, hobby groups, classes. You can also check out the Mindset Matters Hub (details at my website – see page 1), a community that has been created as a place to access resources in the topic areas covered in this book, and connect and learn from others who are on a journey towards thriving in their working lives.

This exercise is very simple – it's all about committing to building community into your life. If you need some pointers about where to start, consider exploring group opportunities in areas of:

- professional interest
- personal interest
- skills you would like to build
- career transitions
- career development

The important focus of a group is belonging, support and connection. When you're part of a community, you're likely to feel that you have a sense of meaning, working towards similar goals with others. It may take a while to find a community where you feel comfortable and connected, and it can take some effort. If building community is important to you, you need to commit to exploring different communities, potentially pushing yourself outside of your comfort zone. If in doubt about where to start, you could explore the Mindset Matters community to see if it's a fit for you at at my website (see page 1).

Ask yourself:

- What do I want to achieve from building a community?
- How have I built community this week?
- How could I invest more in community?

When you find a community that creates belonging for you, you'll be able to authentically be yourself. Often when you join a community, it feels like you're with your kind of people, potentially your tribe. Your community can help you find meaning and help you to reach goals that are important to you.

In the next chapter we'll explore how to weave together all the themes covered in this book to create a strategy that helps you to navigate challenges, change and unpredictability at work. And rather than simply survive these events, we'll focus on how you can create a mindset and way of thinking that helps you to thrive, no matter what situations you may face in the future.

CHAPTER 12

Where do we go from here?

We know we need to expect change, ambiguity, and uncertainty in the workplace of the future, but that doesn't mean we find a complex and challenging working environment desirable. In fact, often it's the case that the more uncertainty we face, the more we crave certainty. How can we change this?

It might be helpful to change the way we view a complex and changeable workplace. If this is the norm now, and likely to continue, we need to shift our thinking to acknowledge that our working environments are no more complex, ambiguous, or changeable than they have been over the last few years. Of course, new challenges will arise, and potentially quickly. But remember, in 2020 and 2021 we dealt with collective change like we've never seen before, and we learned how to navigate that extreme change. Was it desirable? No. Was it comfortable? I'm sure for most of us it wasn't a comfortable experience learning to react so quickly, while trying to grasp an understanding of so many unknown factors. But we did it. If you weren't part of the workforce when the world plunged into an intense experiment and we were all forced to live and work through change at a scale most of us haven't witnessed previously, you can still take lessons from this – use it as a case study.

We can't sugar-coat the psychological impact extreme change can cause. And we also can't confuse coping and reacting to a challenging situation with thriving. But we can learn lessons about ourselves and the environment around us, and if we focus on developing the skills we need to thrive at work in the future (especially in uncertainty), rather than trying to predict exactly how the world of work will change, the focus is shifted from what we can't control – uncertainty – towards what we can – developing skills to help us thrive in *any* changeable situations.

Learning from the past

You have the potential to continually develop the way you think and process information – your mindset has the potential to be agile. You can take control to create a mindset to thrive, even in challenging situations. Although our current realities at work are unlikely to match our experiences in the past, that doesn't mean there's no value in looking back and learning from your past successes and mistakes. Take some time to consider what you've learned about yourself throughout your career:

- How do you react to challenges?
- When do you perform at your best?
- Have you ever reached peak performance? When and how?
- How do you feel about uncertainty?
- What motivates you at work?
- What worries you about work?

Your past leaves clues about who you are, how you process information, and how you interact with the world around you. I hope reading this book has helped you to reflect on these parts of your past career, but there's no limit to how often you take part in this reflection. You may find you uncover different clues each time you reflect. If you'd like to continue this journey of learning about yourself at work, particularly in the context of the skills we need to thrive in the future, here are the chapters to jump back into:

- Chapter 2: Resilience
- Chapter 4: Cognitive flexibility
- Chapter 6: Growth mindset
- Chapter 8: Emotional intelligence
- Chapter 10: Connection

This book is your manual to help you prepare yourself for the future of work. Use it in a way that works for you. Go back to the parts you want to understand in more detail or go back to the chapters about the skills you want to focus on right now.

Taking control of your career today

If you find yourself thinking you have no idea where to go from here, I hope you feel reassured to know *everyone* feels like this at one time or another. Others may appear to have their working lives in order and know exactly what they're doing, and what they need to do next, but we all get stuck. We all have obstacles to overcome. We all have change to navigate.

You can learn to take control of dealing with complex and uncertain environments by working on the skills you need to navigate change effectively. Each of the coaching chapters are full of coaching exercises and strategies designed to help you develop a particular skill. I suggest working on chapters and skills in an order that works for you – start with those that stand out for you. As a reminder, Table 12.1 contains a list of the coaching chapters, and the coaching exercises included in each chapter, which you can tick off as you try them. You can also add notes to keep track of what you've tried and how it works for you, and any tweaks you've made to the exercise.

Choosing your future

As with navigating any new situations, support and connection with others on a similar journey can be the difference between thriving and simply surviving. The

Mindset Matters Hub has been created to help support you on your ongoing mindset mastery journey, and can be accessed at my website (see page 1).

The Hub is full of tools, advice, on-demand courses, downloadable documents and access to live coaching events. Maybe most importantly, the Mindset Matters Hub is somewhere you can access support and connection both with those who are also working on creating a mindset that helps them to thrive, and with experts and coaches who can help facilitate this.

I hope this book serves as one of the tools in your toolbox to help you confidently navigate change and overcome obstacles in your working life. I'm under no illusion that this is an easy process, or that I have all the answers for you. You and your journey are unique. I do, however, hope this book provides help, guidance and a form of support as you navigate the wild ride that is the workplace of the future. On the days where you feel like you just can't work it all out, remember that's part of the process of change – it's not you (I have many days when I feel like this). Come back to this book, check in with the community, look after yourself and know that you can find a way to keep moving forward, even if it's a meandering road to get where you're going, or you need to make a detour, or when you make a few mistakes along the way.

Once you start to change how you look at the new and complex world of work and understand that it can all be an experiment – you don't need to have all the answers, you just need to try *something* and learn along the way – change becomes less daunting. Change is inevitable, uncertainty isn't in your control, but ultimately, when it comes to thriving at work, it's your mindset that matters.

TABLE 12.1   Exercise checklist

	Notes
Chapter 3 Resilience	
Make sense with your senses	....
Confidence weekly reflection	....
Flexible thinking	....
Gratitude	....
Detecting root cause	....
Finding flow	....
Building a board of supporters	....

TABLE 12.1 *continued*

Chapter 5 Mental agility

Reframing thoughts

....

Observe your thoughts

....

Busting confirmation bias

....

Nurture a curious mindset

....

Embrace novelty

....

Strategizing new solutions

....

Chapter 7 Growth mindset

Mindset identifier

....

Continuous improvement

....

Belief

....

TABLE 12.1 *continued*

Add 'yet' to your story ....

Failing forward ....

The challenge ....

Chapter 9 Emotional intelligence

Personal reflection ....

Gathering feedback ....

Breathing ....

Make sense with your senses ....

Intent and impact reflection ....

Interacting with empathy ....

TABLE 12.1 *continued*

Chapter 11 Connection

Connection mapping ....

Building connected relationships ....

Value identifier ....

Micro-meaning moment ....

Setting values-based goals ....

Building community ....

Notes

Introduction

1 A Grant. There's a name for the blah you're feeling: It's called languishing, *New York Times*, 19 April 2021, www.nytimes.com/2021/04/19/well/mind/covid-mental-health-languishing.html (archived at https://perma.cc/5ZX9-ALZV)

Chapter 1 We've come a long way

1 BBC. French workers get 'right to disconnect' from emails out of hours, BBC, 31 December 2016, www.bbc.co.uk/news/world-europe-38479439 (archived at https://perma.cc/6J5L-2MS4); A Matei. Portugal banned bosses from texting employees after work. Could it happen in the US?, *Guardian*, 15 November 2021, www.theguardian.com/lifeandstyle/2021/nov/15/portugal-boss-texts-work-us-employment (archived at https://perma.cc/X7Q9-N36Y)

2 B Rosso, K Dekas and A Wrzesniewski. On the meaning of work: A theoretical integration and review, *Research in Organizational Behavior*, 2010, 30, 91–127

3 C Mui. How Kodak failed, Forbes, 18 January 2012, www.forbes.com/sites/chunkamui/2012/01/18/how-kodak-failed (archived at https://perma.cc/2LZK-MVUF)

4 DBS. DBS is World's Best Bank for third year in a row, 2019, www.dbs.com/newsroom/DBS_Worlds_Best_Bank_for_third_year_in_a_row (archived at https://perma.cc/57XT-UNJP)

5 M Zahn and A Serwer. Netflix co-founder on creative culture: We 'manage on the edge of chaos', Yahoo Finance, 8 September 2020, https://finance.yahoo.com/news/netflix-cofounder-reed-hastings-on-creative-culture-130348112.html (archived at https://perma.cc/94VP-TPY2)

---

6 A Ash, The rise and fall of Blockbuster and how it's surviving with just
one store left, Business Insider, 12 August 2020, www.businessinsider.
com/the-rise-and-fall-of-blockbuster-video-streaming-2020-1 (archived
at https://perma.cc/8FHA-7A8F)

Chapter 2 Resilience

1 N Garmezy. Resilience in children's adaptation to negative life events
and stressed environments, *Pediatric Annals*, 1991, 20 (9), 459–66;
A Masten, K Best and N Garmezy. Resilience and development:
Contributions from the study of children who overcome adversity,
Development and Psychopathology, 1990, 2 (4), 425–44; S Luthar,
D Cicchetti and B Becker. The construct of resilience: A critical evaluation
and guidelines for future work, *Child Development*, 2000, 71 (3),
543–62; A Masten and A Narayan. Child development in the context of
disaster, war, and terrorism: Pathways of risk and resilience, *Annual
Review of Psychology*, 2012, 63, 227–57
2 M Seery. Resilience: A silver lining to experiencing adverse life events?
Current Directions in Psychological Science, 2011, 20 (6), 390–94
3 D Elliott. 6 things to know about the future of skills and workplace
learning, World Economic Forum, 1 June 2021, www.weforum.org/
agenda/2021/06/workplace-skills-learning-linkedin-report/ (archived at
https://perma.cc/2UMA-63AL)
4 J Griffith and C West. Master resilience training and its relationship to
individual well-being and stress buffering among Army National Guard
soldiers, *The Journal of Behavioral Health Services and Research*, 2013,
40 (2), 140–55
5 J Ayala and G Manzano. The resilience of the entrepreneur: Influence on
the success of the business: A longitudinal analysis, *Journal of Economic
Psychology*, 2014, 42, 126–35
6 D Fletcher and M Sarkar. A grounded theory of psychological resilience
in Olympic champions, *Psychology of Sport and Exercise*, 2012, 13 (5),
669–78
7 M Zetlin. Elon Musk says anyone can learn to innovate by asking 3
simple questions, Inc., 12 December 2020, www.inc.com/minda-zetlin/

elon-musk-innovation-innovate-tesla-spacex-wall-street-journal-interview-matt-murray.html (archived at https://perma.cc/ES4F-96S4)

8 D Straus. The genius problem-solving method Elon Musk learned from Aristotle, Inc., 12 July 2017, www.inc.com/david-straus/the-genius-problem-solving-method-elon-musk-learne.html (archived at https://perma.cc/7F3X-HKQN)

9 Innomind. The first principles method explained by Elon Musk (online video), 2013, www.youtube.com/watch?v=NV3sBlRgzTI (archived at https://perma.cc/EPS6-7QSF)

10 A Pangallo, L Zibarras, R Lewis and P Flaxman. Resilience through the lens of interactionism: A systematic review, *Psychological Assessment*, 2015, 27 (1), 1

11 C Waugh and E Koster. A resilience framework for promoting stable remission from depression, *Clinical Psychology Review*, 2015, 41, 49–60

12 E Kleiman, A Chiara, R Liu, S Jager-Hyman, J Choi and L Alloy. Optimism and well-being: A prospective multi-method and multi-dimensional examination of optimism as a resilience factor following the occurrence of stressful life events, *Cognition and Emotion*, 2017, 31(2), 269–83

13 M Seligman (2004) *Authentic Happiness: Using the new positive psychology to realize your potential for lasting fulfilment*, Simon and Schuster, New York

14 R Kalisch, M Müller and O Tüscher. A conceptual framework for the neurobiological study of resilience, *Behavioral and Brain Sciences*, 2015, 38

15 C Gallo. How James Dyson's thousands of failures can help you tell a captivating founder origin story, Inc., 9 September 2021, www.inc.com/carmine-gallo/how-james-dysons-thousands-of-failures-can-help-you-tell-a-captivating-founder-origin-story.html (archived at https://perma.cc/898H-43NW)

16 E Woo. Herbert Hyman dies at 82; founder of Coffee Bean & Tea Leaf chain, *LA Times*, 3 May 2014, www.latimes.com/local/obituaries/la-me-herb-hyman-20140504-story.html (archived at https://perma.cc/RQ5R-F285)

17 J Davis. How Lego clicked: The super brand that reinvented itself, *Guardian*, 4 June 2017, www.theguardian.com/lifeandstyle/2017/jun/04/

how-lego-clicked-the-super-brand-that-reinvented-itself (archived at
https://perma.cc/P2GQ-M47X)

18 M Seery and W Quinton (2016) Understanding resilience: From
negative life events to everyday stressors, in *Advances in Experimental
Social Psychology: Vol 54*, Academic Press, Cambridge, MA, 181–245

19 M Csikszentmihalyi (1990) *Flow: The psychology of optimal experience*,
Harper and Row, New York City

20 S Sandberg and A Grant (2017) *Option B: Facing adversity, building
resilience, and finding joy*, Michel Lafon, New York City

21 M Bernabé and J Botia. Resilience as a mediator in emotional social
support's relationship with occupational psychology health in
firefighters, *Journal of Health Psychology*, 2016, 21 (8), 1778–86

22 A Pangallo, L Zibarras, R Lewis and P Flaxman. Resilience through the
lens of interactionism: A systematic review, *Psychological Assessment*,
2015, 27 (1), 1

23 M Rutter. Resilience as a dynamic concept, *Development and
Psychopathology*, 2012, 24 (2), 335–44

24 G Werther. Resilience: Its conceptual links to creating society-specific
forecasts about emerging change, *Armed Forces and Society*, 2014,
40 (3), 428–51

Chapter 3 Coaching: Bouncing forward

1 M Csikszentmihalyi (1990) *Flow: The psychology of optimal experience*,
Harper and Row, New York City

Chapter 4 Cognitive flexibility

1 S Gosling, P Rentfrow and W Swann Jr. A very brief measure of the
big-five personality domains, *Journal of Research in Personality*, 2003,
37 (6), 504–28

2 M Neenan and W Dryden (2013) *Life Coaching: A cognitive-
behavioural approach*, Routledge, London

3 F Ruiz. Acceptance and commitment therapy versus traditional cognitive
behavioral therapy: A systematic review and meta-analysis of current

empirical evidence, *International Journal of Psychology and Psychological Therapy*, 2012, 12 (3), 333–57

4 R Harris (2008) *The Happiness Trap: Stop struggling, start living*, Constable and Robinson, London

5 R Gillett. How Walt Disney, Oprah Winfrey, and 19 other successful people rebounded after getting fired, Inc., 7 October 2015, www.inc.com/ business-insider/21-successful-people-who-rebounded-after-getting-fired.html (archived at https://perma.cc/25RX-LPRH)

6 W Isaacson (2011) *Steve Jobs by Walter Isaacson: The exclusive biography*, Simon and Schuster, New York City

7 Fortune. The world's 50 greatest leaders, 2017, https://fortune.com/ worlds-greatest-leaders/2017/ (archived at https://perma.cc/7LSK-JN3R)

8 D Clark (2016) *Alibaba: The house that Jack Ma built*, Ecco, New York City

9 A Montag. Billionaire Alibaba founder Jack Ma was rejected from every job he applied to after college, even KFC, CNBC, 10 August 2017, www.cnbc.com/2017/08/09/lesson-alibabas-jack-ma-learned-after-being-rejected-for-a-job-at-kfc.html (archived at https://perma.cc/9QUM-KMXH)

10 O Winfrey. Wellesley College commencement address, 30 May 1997, www.wellesley.edu/events/commencement/archives/1997commencement/ commencementaddress (archived at https://perma.cc/GV9U-83EN)

Chapter 5 Coaching: The art of the everyday pivot

1 G Roberts (2021) Mindset Matters, LinkedIn, www.linkedin.com/ newsletters/mindset-matters-6661628561960558592/ (archived at https://perma.cc/A3NF-ALFU)

Chapter 6 A growth mindset

1 C Dweck (2008) *Mindset: The new psychology of success*, Random House Digital, Inc, New York City

2 A Hochanadel and D Finamore. Fixed and growth mindset in education and how grit helps students persist in the face of adversity, *Journal of*

International Education Research, 2015, 11 (1), 47–50; J Sarrasin, L Nenciovici, L Foisy, G Allaire-Duquette, M Riopel and S Masson. Effects of teaching the concept of neuroplasticity to induce a growth mindset on motivation, achievement, and brain activity: A meta-analysis, *Trends in Neuroscience and Education*, 2018, 12, 22–31

3 S Shibu and S Lebowitz. Microsoft is rolling out a new management framework to its leaders. It centers around a psychological insight called growth mindset, Business Insider, 11 November 2019, www.businessinsider.com/microsoft-is-using-growth-mindset-to-power-management-strategy-2019-11 (archived at https://perma.cc/E26K-HEBZ)

4 H Schroder, M Yalch, S Dawood, C Callahan, M Donnellan and J Moser. Growth mindset of anxiety buffers the link between stressful life events and psychological distress and coping strategies, *Personality and Individual Differences*, 2017, 110, 23–26

5 Geekwire. Jeff Bezos shares his management style and philosophy (online video), 2016, www.youtube.com/watch?v=F7JMMy-yHSU (archived at https://perma.cc/R9EW-8458)

6 M Syed (2010) *Bounce: The myth of talent and the power of practice*, HarperCollins, London

7 D Elliott. 6 things to know about the future of skills and workplace learning, World Economic Forum, 1 June 2021, www.weforum.org/agenda/2021/06/workplace-skills-learning-linkedin-report/ (archived at https://perma.cc/2UMA-63AL)

8 M Obama (2018) *Becoming*, Viking, New York

9 Forbes. The richest in 2021, www.forbes.com/billionaires/ (archived at https://perma.cc/7T3J-QQXF)

10 T James. Like all great innovators, Amazon's Bezos unfazed by recent failures, Wired, 2015, www.wired.com/insights/2015/02/like-all-great-innovators-amazons-bezos-unfazed-by-recent-failures/ (archived at https://perma.cc/RPS8-BRTA)

11 K Majdan and M Wasowski. We sat down with Microsoft's CEO to discuss the past, present and future of the company, Business Insider, 20 April 2017, www.businessinsider.com/satya-nadella-microsoft-ceo-qa-2017-4?r=US&IR=T (archived at https://perma.cc/A4YN-RW44)

12 M Burton. By learning from failures, Lilly keeps drug pipeline full, *The Wall Street Journal*, 21 April 2004, www.wsj.com/articles/SB108249266648388235 (archived at https://perma.cc/2PYB-44XX)

13 H Taneja. The era of 'move fast and break things' is over, Harvard Business Review, 22 January 2019, https://hbr.org/2019/01/the-era-of-move-fast-and-break-things-is-over (archived at https://perma.cc/X9XH-HQG3)

14 J Bezos. Amazon, 1997. www.sec.gov/Archives/edgar/data/1018724/000119312516530910/d168744dex991.htm (archived at https://perma.cc/2VPH-WHHT)

15 E Catmull (2014) *Creativity Inc.*, Bantam Press, New York

16 Creativity Inc. Build a successful creative culture with 7 core principles from Pixar, 2021, www.creativityincbook.com/7-core-principles/ (archived at https://perma.cc/2HR8-QDFV)

17 A Edmondson (2018) *The Fearless Organization: Creating psychological safety in the workplace for learning, innovation, and growth*, Wiley, Hoboken

18 D Yeager and C Dweck. Mindsets that promote resilience: When students believe that personal characteristics can be developed, *Educational Psychologist*, 2012, 47 (4), 302–14

19 I Robertson, C Cooper, M Sarkar and T Curran. Resilience training in the workplace from 2003 to 2014: A systematic review, *Journal of Occupational and Organizational Psychology*, 2015, 88 (3), 533–62

Chapter 7 Coaching: Learning forward

1 McKinsey & Company. The work of leaders in a lean management enterprise, 2017, www.mckinsey.com/business-functions/operations/our-insights/the-work-of-leaders-in-a-lean-management-enterprise (archived at https://perma.cc/6MYP-MG23)

Chapter 8 Emotional intelligence

1 G Roberts. Developing your emotional intelligence, LinkedIn Learning, 23 May 2017, www.linkedin.com/learning/developing-your-emotional-intelligence/what-are-the-benefits-of-emotional-intelligence? (archived at https://perma.cc/NHQ7-5BE9)

2 A Schlaerth, N Ensari and J Christian. A meta-analytical review of the relationship between emotional intelligence and leaders' constructive conflict management, *Group Processes and Intergroup Relations*, 2013, 16 (1), 126–36

3 L Barrett (2017) *How Emotions Are Made: The secret life of the brain*, Houghton Mifflin, Boston

4 D Goleman (1996) *Emotional Intelligence: Why it can matter more than IQ*, Bloomsbury, London

5 Harvard Business Review. Leading by feel, 2004, 82 (1), 27, https://hbr.org/2004/01/leading-by-feel (archived at https://perma.cc/6D54-T6YM)

6 NPR. Understanding unconscious bias (podcast), 15 July 2020, www.npr.org/2020/07/14/891140598/understanding-unconscious-bias?t=1638292012086 (archived at https://perma.cc/G7WB-BME2)

7 Harvard Business Review. Leading by feel, 2004, 82 (1), 27, https://hbr.org/2004/01/leading-by-feel (archived at https://perma.cc/6D54-T6YM)

8 M Cole, J Cox and J Stavros. Building collaboration in teams through emotional intelligence: Mediation by SOAR (strengths, opportunities, aspirations, and results), *Journal of Management and Organization*, 2019, 25 (2), 263–83

9 B Mekpor and K Dartey-Baah. Beyond the job description: Exploring the mediating role of leaders' emotional intelligence on the nexus between leadership styles and voluntary workplace behaviours in the Ghanaian banking sector, *Journal of Management Development*, 2020, 39 (2), 240–52

10 M Cole, J Cox and J Stavros. Building collaboration in teams through emotional intelligence: Mediation by SOAR (strengths, opportunities, aspirations, and results), *Journal of Management and Organization*, 2019, 25 (2), 263–83

11 S Hendriani. The influence of emotional intelligence on team performance through knowledge sharing, team conflict, and the structure mechanism, *Journal of Management Development*, 2020, 39 (3), 269–92

12 S Krishnakumar, B Perera, K Hopkins and M Robinson. On being nice and effective: Work-related emotional intelligence and its role in conflict resolution and interpersonal problem-solving, *Conflict Resolution Quarterly*, 2019, 37 (2), 147–67

13 C Lee and C Wong. The effect of team emotional intelligence on team process and effectiveness, *Journal of Management and Organization*, 2019, 25 (6), 844–59

14 A Schlaerth, N Ensari and J Christian. A meta-analytical review of the relationship between emotional intelligence and leaders' constructive conflict management, *Group Processes and Intergroup Relations*, 2013, 16 (1), 126–36

15 A D'Amico, A Geraci and C Tarantino. The relationship between perceived emotional intelligence, work engagement, job satisfaction, and burnout in Italian school teachers: An exploratory study, *Psihologijske teme*, 2020, 29 (1), 63–84

16 S Dilawar, D Durrani, X Li and M Anjum. Decision-making in highly stressful emergencies: The interactive effects of trait emotional intelligence, *Current Psychology*, 2021, 40 (6), 2988–3005

17 N Schutte, J Malouff, E Thorsteinsson, N Bhullar and S Rooke. A meta-analytic investigation of the relationship between emotional intelligence and health, *Personality and Individual Differences*, 2007, 42 (6), 921–33

18 M Sadovyy, M Sánchez-Gómez and E Bresó. Covid-19: How the stress generated by the pandemic may affect work performance through the moderating role of emotional intelligence, *Personality and Individual Differences*, 2021, 180, 110986

19 K Pekaar, A Bakker, D Van der Linden, M Born and H Sirén. Managing own and others' emotions: A weekly diary study on the enactment of emotional intelligence, *Journal of Vocational Behavior*, 2018, 109, 137–51

20 J Grobelny, P Radke and D Paniotova-Maczka. Emotional intelligence and job performance: A meta-analysis, *International Journal of Work Organisation and Emotion*, 2021, 12 (1), 1–47

Chapter 9 Coaching: Interacting with the world

1 A Huberman. How to control stress in real-time: Huberman Lab quantal clip (online video), 2021, www.youtube.com/watch?v=PZ-GvIOhcf8 (archived at https://perma.cc/RB9Z-63MH)

Chapter 10: Connection

1 T Wilhelmsen. How to create a culture of collaboration in the workplace, Great Place to Work, 2 May 2019, www.greatplacetowork.com/resources/blog/how-to-create-a-culture-of-collaboration-in-the-workplace (archived at https://perma.cc/5ABR-XRYX)

2 M Lieberman (2013) *Social: Why our brains are wired to connect*, OUP, Oxford

3 C Ryan. 'Be human': Why Bento for Business built its culture around personal relationships, Built in Chicago, 29 August 2018, www.builtinchicago.org/2018/08/29/spotlight-working-at-bento-for-business (archived at https://perma.cc/RUZ3-9TN9)

4 T Wilhelmsen. How to create a culture of collaboration in the workplace, Great Place to Work, 2 May 2019, www.greatplacetowork.com/resources/blog/how-to-create-a-culture-of-collaboration-in-the-workplace (archived at https://perma.cc/5ABR-XRYX)

5 T Burrows. Workday: Culture is at the heart of digital transformation, ITWeb, 15 April 2021, www.itweb.co.za/content/mYZRXM9aZegMOgA8 (archived at https://perma.cc/8GYL-WW8D)

6 J Kohner. The real meaning behind 'Salesforce community', Salesforce, 6 February 2017, www.salesforce.com/blog/what-is-salesforce-ohana/ (archived at https://perma.cc/R9NP-VESN)

7 Business Roundtable. Business roundtable redefines the purpose of a corporation to promote 'an economy that serves all Americans', 2019, www.businessroundtable.org/business-roundtable-redefines-the-purpose-of-a-corporation-to-promote-an-economy-that-serves-all-americans (archived at https://perma.cc/ZT9N-79FR)

8 A Zapulla. The future of business? Purpose, not just profit, World Economic Forum, 17 January 2019, www.weforum.org/agenda/2019/01/why-businesses-must-be-driven-by-purpose-as-well-as-profits/ (archived at https://perma.cc/2QK7-J5L8)

9 A Alimujiang, A Wiensch, J Boss, N Fleischer, A Mondul, K McLean, B Mukherjee and C Pearce. Association between life purpose and mortality among US adults older than 50 years, *JAMA Network Open*, 2019, 2 (5), e194270

10 T Erickson. Meaning is the new money, *Harvard Business Review*, 23 March 2011, https://hbr.org/2011/03/challenging-our-deeply-held-as (archived at https://perma.cc/K96K-R8BC)

11 S Achor, A Reece, G Kellerman and A Robichaux. 9 out of 10 people are willing to earn less money to do more-meaningful work, *Harvard Business Review*, 6 November 2018, https://hbr.org/2018/11/9-out-of-10-people-are-willing-to-earn-less-money-to-do-more-meaningful-work (archived at https://perma.cc/TK3W-XCKN)

12 DSM. About DSM, 2021, www.dsm.com/corporate/about.html (archived at https://perma.cc/V2AJ-3CY5)

13 DSM. *Royal DSM: Growth and value: Purpose led, performance driven*, October 2018, www.dsm.com/content/dam/dsm/corporate/en_US/documents/dsm-purpose-book-creating-brighter-lives-for-all.pdf (archived at https://perma.cc/76BH-PTNM)

Chapter 11 Coaching: The meaning of connection

1 G Roberts. Mindset Matters interview edition: Setting goals with purpose with Richard McKinnon (online video) 7 October 2021, www.youtube.com/watch?v=9ulrxNqqfis (archived at https://perma.cc/QB7Y-AL7K)

Index

Bold page numbers indicate figures, *italic* numbers indicate tables.

Praise for *Mindset Matters*

"Gemma Leigh Roberts has written a clear, accessible and evidence-based book for anyone who wants to get more out of life. Covering theory and practical application, she gives the reader the insights they need to make transformative changes. Roberts has identified some key and impactful areas, like resilience, relationships and emotional intelligence, which play a huge role in determining how we navigate the challenges of the 21st century. Each is explored and explained with clarity and then turned into practical coaching exercises for the reader. A great addition to anyone's personal development toolkit!" RICHARD A MACKINNON, MANAGING DIRECTOR, WORKLIFEPSYCH

"We are living and working in a fast-changing world where ambiguity and uncertainty are our companions. This demands so much from us, and just as we exercise our muscles to stay physically strong and healthy, there is as much of a need to exercise our mental muscles for mental strength, resilience and health. Gemma Leigh Robert's deep expertise, the research explored, and the practical guides will help you think about how to exercise your mindset, as mindset matters!" JOHANNA BOLIN TINGVALL, GLOBAL HEAD OF GREENHOUSE (L&D), TALENT GROWTH AND COMMUNITYX, SPOTIFY

"When it comes to thriving in the new world of work, your mindset is the number one predictor of success.

Gemma Leigh Roberts has written a book that is the equivalent of checking in with your executive coach – she expertly guides you through coaching strategies to create an impact in your life, all supported by her research and experience as a business psychologist. This book will be your mindset manual to guide you through the new world of work, helping you to build the critical skills you need to thrive." KIM KAUPE, FOUNDER AT BRIGHT IDEAS ONLY

"Everyone needs to buy this book and then read it at least once a year. It is the perfect blend between rigorously researched evidence-based insights combined with being your personal coach. If you do what Gemma Leigh Roberts says in these pages you will build your cognitive flexibility. Which is one of the best gifts you can give yourself in life." AMY BRANN, DIRECTOR OF SYNAPTIC POTENTIAL AND AUTHOR OF *MAKE YOUR BRAIN WORK*, *NEUROSCIENCE FOR COACHES* AND *ENGAGED*